POWER FOR GOD'S SAKE

POWER FOR GOD'S SAKE
Power and abuse
in the local church

Paul Beasley-Murray

paternoster press

Copyright © 1998 Paul Beasley-Murray

First published in 1998 by Paternoster Press

04 03 02 01 99 98   7 6 5 4 3 2 1

Paternoster Press is an imprint of Paternoster Publishing,
PO Box 300, Carlisle, Cumbria, CA3 0QS, UK
http://www.paternoster-publishing.com

British Library Cataloguing in Publication Data
A catalogue record for this book is available from the British Library.

ISBN 0-85364-899-9

Cover design by Mainstream, Lancaster.
Typeset by WestKey Ltd, Falmouth, Cornwall.
Printed in Great Britain by Mackays of Chatham PLC, Kent.

This book is dedicated to
Ian Ainsworth Smith
Martin and Angela Wake
Sister Margaret Magdalen
Morgan Derham
and Margaret Bowker,
with gratitude for their support.

Contents

Acknowledgements

I am greatly indebted to a number of friends who have in various ways assisted in the writing of this book. In particular I wish to acknowledge the help of:

Bert Thrift and Linda Jones and Partners – particularly for their technical expertise. Without them the project would never have been possible.

Tim Rose – for his generosity in underwriting the not inconsiderable cost of the survey; also for his provision of a quiet refuge in the initial stages of drafting the book.

The members of Victoria Road South Baptist Church, Chelmsford – for their kindness in giving me time to engage in research and writing.

Martyn Percy – for his stimulation and encouragement; also for his offer to write the Foreword.

Alan and Ursula Franklin – for their provision of a most comfortable retreat in the closing stages of writing the book.

Last but not least – Caroline, my wife – for her love and patience throughout the writing of this book.

Foreword

We all have experiences of power in one way or another. Language, concepts and encounters with power are a part of everyday life. Some may wield power, others may find themselves under it; some may think they know what the power of the church is, or claim to know the power of God directly. Can any book look at something that is so often taken for granted, and illuminate the subject? Indeed, what would a study of power tell us about ourselves, our theology, the religion to which we might subscribe, or to the one from which we readily flee?

Putting the issue in perspective, we can see how important the issue is if we turn to politics. Within a few days of taking office, Tony Blair was being accused by the Opposition of having become 'power-mad'. The occasion for the accusation was his transformation of Prime Minister's question time. The reactions ranged from allegations of arrogance to amateur diagnoses of megalomania. To be sure, the change in format of Prime Minister's question time appears to have been achieved with the minimum of consultation. Those who revelled in the 'bear pit' atmosphere of the House of Commons on Tuesdays and Thursdays would now have less baying to do. The media, who fed off these regular and occasionally salutary encounters, were quick to express their reservations.

Yet behind this 'story' lies a deep and serious issue over the nature and exercise of power. The reduction in the number of 'open season' encounters a Prime Minister was now subject to in the Commons was seen by some as a retreat from democracy. Others felt that it represented a lack of accountability. From a different perspective, the Prime Minister's question time was viewed by others as near pure theatre, and the time given over to the sessions was actually trivializing the parliamentary process. In other words, too much accountability over so many issues was actually obstructing governance and the overall effectiveness of a democratic programme.

Churches and their leaders are not immune from these dynamics, and Paul Beasley-Murray's timely book explores the relationship between the power in churches and those who wield it. There is much food for thought here. What kind of 'power model' does Jesus connote to the would-be church leader? If a church is absolutist in its testimony to the power of God, does it follow that in its ecclesial formation the maxim 'absolute power corrupts absolutely' will eventually describe the leadership? How can churches be empowered by individuals without being overpowered by the same? What forms of theological and practical discernment can be brought to bear on issues of power?

This book sets out to discuss the diversity and digressions of power from a first-hand perspective, but backed by some empirical research. The book focuses on the church, or rather, churches, as the title – *Power for God's Sake* – is intended to convey the point that there is not just one 'church' to discuss in relation to power. Different ecclesial bodies handle power in different ways, and the powers themselves encountered therein are often quite different. Yet all churches are subject to that subtle relationship between human controls and the divine mandates from which they are said to come. Power is something that is necessarily used, and sometimes abused, in all churches.

There is nothing remarkable about these observations. Power in the church is both medicine and poison. The key to its rightful deployment depends on discernment, diagnosis and dosage. In its relationship to authority, order, charisma or revelation, the identity and concept of 'power' is often lost in a confusing disarray of side-effects. Paul Beasley-Murray's book is a helpful corrective here, and it brings us back to one of the most fundamental and central themes in the Christian life. Without power there is no church, no witness, and nothing to witness to. Yet there is an irony here for the Christian, for the one who stands at the centre of all power demonstrated this by abrogating power, 'giving himself up to death'. So this is a necessarily sensitive and costly book to write, and to read. It is a call for the discernment and dispersal of power, for its redistribution, and for the naming of false and abusive powers. At the same time, it is not naïve, and recognizes that ecclesial communities function with and for power – for God's sake.

An extraordinary feature of life in the late twentieth century is the amount of power that individuals can exert over one another. The nature of power often hides this. An apparently harmless and potentially empowering exercise such as a staff appraisal can quickly become disempowering through an indifferent assessment. The inability to listen to new and constructive ideas or consult with fellow workers can perplex and bewilder a workforce. Equally, power vacuums can create manifold problems, sometimes resulting in more serious difficulties than might arise from a single abusive manager. In political and ecclesial situations, it is sometimes better to have the devil you know rather than the seven you don't (*Matthew* 12:43–45).

All leaders in churches bear a serious responsibility here, and a charge. Beyond the immediate tasks of priesthood, pastoring, ministering or management, there has to be some reckoning with the revelation of God's power in Jesus Christ. This is sometimes in word and in deed – quite compelling. Yet it is never constraining in the sense that no-one is forced to have faith because of an encounter, or because of what they have witnessed. One of the intriguing features of Jesus' ministry and his handling of power is that people are given the space to respond at their own pace and in their own way. Indeed, such is God's respect for created order and humanity that we are even allowed to reject Jesus, and to divest him of the most basic and precious power of all, namely life itself. So Jesus is both a testament to the power of God and also to the willingness of God to give up power. God does not coerce his people, because domination is alien to love. The kind of power God offers and seeks is one that comes through relationality, in which God gives us the space to participate in his life, just as we are, to give him the space that he may participate in ours.

This is why leaders must stay in touch with those they have been called or chosen to lead. A sense of detachment and superiority is a failure of power, and a corruption of authority. Equally, leaders must not become isolated from reality, but rather immersed in it, so that the exercise of power is always relevant and rightful. Power, when exercised, must give space and the possibility for an appropriate response in order that relationships can flourish. Power that does not empower and produce dialogue is on the path to totalitarianism. Leader, beware.

Outside the town of Lewes in Sussex there is a monument built to commemorate Simon de Montfort and his victory over Henry III that laid the foundation for the first parliament in this country. On it is the following inscription: 'Law is like fire, for it lights as truth, warms as charity, burns as zeal. With these virtues as his guide, the king will rule well.' Some kind of rule may well be necessary in all churches, at least until the true kingdom comes. In the meantime, truth, charity, warmth and zeal – these remain the true antidotes to the perils of power.

MARTYN PERCY
Lincoln Institute for the
Study of Religion and Science,
University of Sheffield

Chapter One

Power Abuse in the Church:
Facing up to the Dangerous Reality

1. Dishonesty in high places

> Churches can be cockpits of conflict; deeply neurotic places where
> people play power games and deny the reality of their own circum-
> stances. I have witnessed these things and been part of the strange
> collusion that allows churches to be extremely dishonest places.[1]

Christian people suffer from a considerable degree of naïvety, if not
self-inflicted blindness. We know that power games are a reality in
the world of politics and in the world of business, but we do not
want to accept that they are also a reality in the church. Yet why
should the church be any different from the world in this respect?
If all the other sins of the 'flesh' are to be found in the church, then
why not this one? Any intelligent reading of the New Testament
reveals that there were power struggles right from the beginning of
the life of the early church. One recalls not only James and John,
anxious to sit on the right and left hand of Jesus in his glory, but
also the Judaizers who wanted to impose their way of doing church
on the Gentile converts, the bickering factions at Corinth . . . It is
scarcely an exaggeration to say that within every strand of the New
Testament we can find evidence of power struggles affecting the life

---

[1] Richard Holloway in *Churches and How to Survive Them* (Harper-
Collins, London 1994) by Richard Holloway & Brice Avery, xiv.

of God's people. Yet time and again we seem to close our eyes to this underlying reality, and many of us apparently prefer to live with an 'ideal' picture of the church.

2. Power in the raw

Of course there are overt and organized power struggles in churches which hit the national headlines, and which are therefore widely recognized.

In the North American scene one such public power struggle took place in the early 1990s at First Baptist Church Dallas, described by some as the most influential church in America. *Too Great a Temptation: The Seductive Power of America's Super Church* is the title of the book Joel Gregory wrote after his losing the battle with W.A. Criswell. It's a searingly honest and painful account, revealing the power, the politics and the hypocrisy which plagued that church, as they do many others too. The concluding six pages should be compulsory reading for all church leaders, both ordained and unordained. From his own bitter experience Gregory came to see that

> . . . the church . . . is an institution divine in its original foundation but tethered to this celestial ball by every frailty to which humans are subject. Covetousness, littleness, jealousy, lust for power, ego, sacrilege, and a hundred other demons all lurk within the hallways. . . .
>
> The church on earth at its best is a crippled institution that God may elect to use for his purposes. The divinization of the church in an egotistic triumphalism denigrates the very purpose for which it is founded. After all, its founder died on the cross between two felons. Out of his weakness came strength and out of his death came life. Humanity does not consider Jesus Christ its centerpiece because he behaved like the CEO of a gigantic ecclesiastical corporation. He washed the feet of others; he did not trample them under his own in the name of God.[2]

---

[2] Joel Gregory, *Too Great a Temptation* (The Summit Group, Fort Worth, Texas 1994) 324.

In Britain probably the most well-known power struggle has been the one involving Brandon Jackson, the Dean of Lincoln Cathedral, and the cathedral's canons. Time and again this battle hit the national headlines. Significantly this long-running saga, apparently resolved with the resignation of Brandon Jackson in the summer of 1997, had roots which go way beyond the loss-making exhibition of the cathedral's copy of the Magna Carta in Australia in 1988. According to the official report of Brian Thorne and Kathleen Baker, who were brought in by the Bishop of Lincoln to act as mediators between the protagonists, the conflict, marked by 'the presence of fear and rage within the group and of a sense of intolerable pain', actually has its roots in the distant past. The report speaks of historic myths and 'powerful unconscious forces at work' and says: 'These basic assumptions have probably permeated the Lincoln environment for centuries and they operate in complete opposition to the spirit of the cathedral statutes, which require collegiality and co-operation based on an atmosphere of trust.'[3]

Here is a salutary reminder that unless major power struggles are dealt with, seeds of destructiveness may spill over from one generation to another. To put it in different terms, institutional 'viruses', as it were, can develop, with the result that although the players may change, the struggle does not. Hence the phenomenon, seen in certain local churches, whereby one minister after another leaves that church in unhappy circumstances. There is an abusive corporate mind-set (heart-set?) which desperately needs attention.

But to return to First Baptist, Dallas, and Lincoln Cathedral. Although these churches may be exceptional in the way in which the clerical wrangling has been made so damagingly public, the infighting itself is not so exceptional. Struggles for power and influence are the bread-and-butter diet of many a church, even though such struggles carry pious labels.

Not all power games, of course, involve power struggles between ordained ministers. Such conflicts take place at various levels. For

---

[3] *The Times*, Saturday 30th November 1991.

instance, in some churches ministers are pawns in the hands of their church boards. Gerald Coates, the leader of the 'Pioneer' group of 'New' churches, once caricatured the life of many a Baptist church when he wrote: 'Resist the devil and he will flee from you – resist the deacons and they will fly at you.'[4] As another wit put it, 'Deacons can make even Herod look compassionate!'

Sometimes ministers become the victims of a small but powerful faction within the church. One example of Anglican in-fighting which hit the national press was the power struggle between clergy and laity at Selby Abbey, which brought about the resignation of three vicars within six years. A former Vicar of Selby, Rev Peter Dodd, said: 'At Selby Abbey there is a tiny minority who would appear to be twisting how they would define the will of God to achieve their own personal ends and desire for status. There is a vociferous, small group within the Abbey who are determined to have their own way at whatever personal cost to the vicar.'[5] This Anglican example of clergy victimization can be paralleled many times over in any and every denomination. The only difference between Selby Abbey and other churches is the high profile the struggle received.

On other occasions it is not the ministers, but the members of the church who are abused. They are abused in the sense that power is perverted, people are manipulated, families are divided, and casualties abound. An unhealthy dependence of members on the leadership develops and ultimately creates total spiritual confusion in their lives. The leaders of such churches so mesmerize their followers that, for a while at least, their leadership is accepted without question. One thinks for instance of the People's Temple led by Jim Jones, who was responsible for the suicide and murder of some 900 of his members in Jonestown, Guyana; or of the Branch Davidians led by David Koresh, many of whose adherents died in the siege of Waco in 1993. However, abuses of power are also to be found in more orthodox churches.

---

[4] Gerald Coates, *What on Earth is this Kingdom?* (Kingsway, Eastbourne 1983).

[5] *The Times*, Friday July 12th 1996.

Some of the more charismatic community churches have been particularly prone to authoritarian leadership, manipulation, excessive discipline and spiritual intimidation.[6] An early membership handbook emanating from the 'Harvestime' Restoration group of churches based in Bradford, put submission to the leaders of the church on the same level as submission to God. In this handbook the injunction to 'obey your leaders and submit to them' (Heb. 13:17) was paralleled with James 4:7 which calls Christians to 'submit [themselves] to God' – implying that there is little difference between 'submission' to the elders and 'submission' to God.[7] One obvious difference, of course, is that human leaders are fallible, whereas God is infallible.

Among the main-line churches, one can point to the spellbinding power exercised by the Rev. Chris Brain, the Sheffield vicar who in 1986 set up the rave-style 'Nine o'clock Service' until after revelations of a wide-ranging abuse he was removed from his post in 1995. According to Roland Howard, 'Brain's manipulative techniques with those he was close to were astounding. He had the ability to create slavish dependence even with the strongest, best-balanced and most intelligent people. . . . He oozed charisma, and his jaw-dropping service conferred an aura of mystery and power.'[8]

Sadly, time and again power has been misused and people have been abused in Christian churches and institutions. The travesty is that power has been exercised as though it were for God's sake, even though the real underlying issues may have had nothing to do with God himself. (To be fair, it is not only Christians who have been guilty of acting out of false motives. Members of the helping professions in general can likewise be unconsciously motivated by a lust for power, while appearing to operate under

---

[6] See Ronald M.Enroth, *Churches That Abuse* (Zondervan, Grand Rapids 1992).

[7] *Belonging to an Anointed Body* (privately printed, no date) 20.

[8] Roland Howard, 'The Raving Reverence', *Sunday Times Magazine* 25th August 1996. See also Roland Howard, *The Rise and Fall of the Nine O'Clock Service* (Cassell, London 1996).

a cloak of objective and moral rectitude.)[9] To make matters worse, because Christian faith is a matter of life and death, there is often a peculiar intensity surrounding power and power struggles in the church. The bitterness of Christian in-fighting has to be experienced to be believed. Would that God could at times be left outside the situation!

Many have been deeply wounded. The wounds have been so deep and the pain so intense that large numbers have left the church altogether. Indeed, it is not simply those who have been abused who have left, but also those who have seen friends and loved ones abused. This experience of the abuse of power in the church has been so devastaig that many have given up on God altogether. Others may still retain their faith in God, but although they may not have given up on God, they most certainly have given up on his people. And who would blame them? In the words of one placard: 'Those who make it hardest to be a Christian in this world are often the other Christians.'

Furthermore, such power games within the church have all too often seriously hindered the church in its mission and growth. Writing about the USA, Lyle Schaller, a distinguished American church growth consultant, says that

> . . . on any given day in perhaps three-quarters of all churches the ministry of that congregation is reduced significantly as a result of non-productive conflict. In perhaps one fourth of all churches that internal conflict is so sufficiently severe that it must be reduced before the parish can redirect its energies and resources towards formulating new goals and expanding its ministry.[10]

Indeed, the mission of the church is not just affected by the waste of misdirected and misspent energy. The very fact that power games are being played is a negative witness in itself to those

---

[9] See Adolf Guggenbuehl-Craig, *Power in the Helping Professions* (Spring Publications, Dallas, Texas 1971).
[10] Lyle E.Schaller in the Foreword to *Leadership and Conflict* (Abingdon Press, Nashville 1982) by Speed Leas.

outside the church. Warring and abusive factions in the church undermine the credibility of the Christian faith.

Power for God's sake is a serious problem – and not just in a few isolated spots, but in the church as a whole. Carol McCarthy, an experienced Baptist minister now working within London's inner city, is surely right when she writes:

> I would say that in these days, the big unrecognised temptation in the Church is power. . . . Power is alluring and addictive and some of those who are most susceptible are those most devout and faithful in church work. Once you have had a place in the Church, you can't do without it; once you have had influence, it's hard to withdraw. Those who fain would serve God best may be most deeply wounded. Unless we recognise this and face up to it, life in our churches may be stifled. I don't describe this as a sin but a temptation for those who are tempted to hold on to power, but certainly didn't begin their service with that motivation. Power is captivating and we must wake up to it.[11]

3. The psycho-dynamics of power

The insidious nature of the abuse of power in church life is well illustrated in a powerfully perceptive personal communication sent to me by Carol Bulkeley. Both because she is not a minister and also because of her training in psycho-dynamics, her reflections bring out a dimension of the abuse of power not always fully appreciated by those in church leadership. Although somewhat lengthy, with her permission I reproduce the communication in full:

> The most damaging abuse of power is that which happens unconsciously, whereby those misappropriating the power may well be unaware of their actions or of the repercussions. No one is immune – indeed, quite often it is those who are most well-meaning and

---

[11] Carol McCarthy, 'Ministry In The Local Church', *Baptist Ministers Journal* 250 (April 1955) 16.

concerned for others who fall prey because it is a learnt pattern developed from the primary care-givers around them in their formative years: i.e. the authority figures that made up their childhood in the home, church and school. These are the impressionable foundational years when we absorb unquestioningly the attitudes of those around us, incorporate them into our belief system and only later are able to challenge, review, and reframe if necessary. The difficulty for many of us is that abusive patterns of relating feel 'normal' because, of course, in the world in which we developed that was normal. If such patterns begin to work against us rather than for us, then major rethinking has to happen. The process of challenge and change is demanding and difficult, but opens up vistas of unimagined beauty and joy in relationship, all of which ease the pain involved.

At the heart of all abuse is the misuse of power. It is about relating in ways which in some way diminish the other, rendering them to some degree impotent and powerless. It is about manipulation and control, whereby we have a strong unconscious investment in needing others to share our beliefs. It becomes irrational and important to us that others share and adopt our view – otherwise our defence is threatened and insecurity abounds. We may acknowledge at an intellectual level that difference within the church is a healthy and enriching dynamic, and yet at an emotional level this can feel immensely threatening. The danger for any with positions of power within the church is that it will consciously or otherwise be misused. Few would ever want to – yet it happens.

One of the most subtle and damaging abuses of power is to discourage the thinking capacity within the flock. After all, where there is free thought, anything might happen! It happens through people being told what is acceptable and what isn't, and any errant sheep that deviate by being different soon know they've stepped out of line. Of course it has to be recognised that sheep that stay together, meekly following one another, are very much easier to shepherd, but in the process they lose their individuality. This poses a real dilemma for shepherd and sheep alike. Living under the constraints of control can feel stifling and inhibiting, yet total freedom produces mayhem. Maybe Jesus shows us the way, leading us as he did by love which respected the other and the decisions they chose to make, some of which must have grieved his heart.

Respect is a missing ingredient where the abuse of power is operating – respect for the worth of another and their right to their opinion.

Children who have never been allowed or encouraged to think become robots: i.e. they are obedient compliant children who do whatever they are told out of fear of losing the acceptance they crave, but who in the process lose the capacity to think. They become incapable of making any decisions for fear of getting it wrong, because they've never been allowed or encouraged to – with the result that their own unique potential gets buried deep inside them, lost to themselves and the world at large. These people as adults panic when asked what their opinion is – they honestly do not know, because they've lost the capacity to form an opinion.

Churches – sadly – seem to attract adult-children, searching for a community that feels 'safe' because it replicates the atmosphere of their childhood. All the while they are being told what to do, what's acceptable and what isn't, they feel very safe and secure until through the preaching and teaching they begin to grow up and think. Then the fun really begins! It works both ways – those who want to remain emotionally 'children' feel very threatened as soon as change of any kind is indicated or as soon as they have to make a decision. Equally those who grow in maturity no longer wish to be treated like children, being told what to do. My own view is that we need to lean on the side of encouraging growth and 'hold' the anxieties and fears that growth involves. Hence the importance for people to feel their opinion is valued. Only then do they grow in confidence sufficiently to eventually enable them to take a few risks. We have to create an atmosphere of safety and total acceptance, whereby people will sense at a deep level that their opinion is authentic. Where this is a new experience for some, the fear attached to the vulnerability attached to taking that risk is enormous and cannot be over-estimated. For many the church family may be the first place where they learn 'It's OK to be me'. That is an immense privilege for us, but also an awesome responsibility, to ensure that we don't undermine them. We may not again be given another opportunity to undo the damage. This is after all the unconditional love God extends to us and which we should mirror, but because all of us to a greater or lesser degree grew up never really believing it, it takes us the rest of our lives to get beyond our intellect into our heart and then live in accordance with it.

Very often the abuse of power is seen in only its overt context as physical violence or obvious sexual abuse. Damaging though these manifestations are, in some respects they are less destructive in the sense that they are obvious and recognisable, and if the individuals concerned are able to acknowledge and ask for help, a healing process can be set in motion. However, covert forms of abuse are particularly destructive and damaging, undermining people's integrity and self-worth, causing them to doubt their own reality and perceptions, causing them to deny the validity of their own feelings and insights. Power abuse within the church is like a cancer that devours healthy cells, causing a sickness which if not treated will be 'nigh unto death'. It is a serious problem in any community from the cradle to the grave, which needs to be addressed in the first place through raising the awareness. Otherwise we are perpetually sick communities that are a denial of the life in all its fullness that Jesus embodied. Churches are forever trying to proclaim 'the Good News' – until its members live it and experience it, there's little hope of anyone else believing it.

I suppose a pertinent question church communities need to ask of themselves is: 'Does my experience of God feel like Good News? or does it have more of a feel of a prison sentence about it? and if so does this say something about God and his demands, or is it more about my perception of God? Does my faith liberate, energise and release me, or does it screw me up?' Where faith constricts and binds and paralyses, we need to ask ourselves: 'Whose controlling me – God or others?' So often it seems people are not in fear of God – it's what others will think and that seems endemic in the church.

The abuse of power is about divesting others of their power. It is about situations which seem to provide no choice. Fear and anger will always be around where power abuse is operating and in that climate conditions for personal growth are severely limited. Power abuse, because it robs people of their power to some degree, will to the same degree render people impotent. In bald terms this reduces them to robot-status – which makes for easy shepherding but lonely leadership.

4. The 'power' project

Power is a very real issue for the church. What's more, it is a dangerous issue in the church, precisely because it is all too often unrecognized. It is this conviction which provides the motivation for the writing of this book. Initially I thought that I might detail some of my own experiences of the abuse of power. Some of them are pretty hair-raising! However, fascinating as personal and anecdotal experience may be, it is dangerous to generalize from such experiences.

I looked around to see what people had written on the subject, thinking that I might be able to interact with some of the pertinent literature. To my amazement, within the British scene at least, there was virtually nothing.

In 1986 *The Religion of Power*, a highly readable paperback by Cheryl Forbes, hit the British Christian book shops, but this was in fact a British reprint of an American book first published in 1983.[12] Furthermore, although highly relevant, its primary focus was not on the local church.

In 1983 *Freedom and Discipleship: Your Church and Your Personal Decisions* was published, but the focus here was on church discipline and 'heavy shepherding', and it was concerned primarily with the abuse of power within the renewal movement.[13]

In 1996 Martyn Percy's *Words, Wonders and Power* appeared, but this masterly review of contemporary Christian fundamentalism and revivalism is primarily an analysis of the Wimber phenomenon.[14] Martyn Percy's most recent contribution to the subject of power has been a collection of essays published in 1997 entitled *Power and the Church*,[15] but the focus is more academic in its use of sociology and theology, than an applied study.

---

[12] *The Religion of Power* published in the UK by Marc Europe of Bromley, Kent, was originally published in 1983 by Zondervan.

[13] Jerram Barrs, *Freedom and Discipleship: Your Church and Your Personal Decisions* (IVP, Leicester 1983). In the USA it appeared as *Shepherd and Sheep: a Biblical View of Leading and Following* (IVP, Downers Grove, Illinois 1983).

[14] Martyn Percy, *Words, Wonders and Power: Understanding Contemporary Christian Fundamentalism and Revivalism* (SPCK, London 1996).

[15] Martyn Percy, *Power and the Church: Ecclesiology in an Age of Transition* (Cassell, London 1997).

There seemed to be nothing on the use and abuse of power in the local church, at least not in mainstream church life. This conclusion was confirmed after I had spent a number of days during the summer of 1995 combing the resources of the Cambridge University Library. It became clear that this is virgin territory as far as Britain is concerned. No serious work has been done in this area.

In the light of all this I realized that if I were to make a contribution, then, instead of relying on my own experience, I needed to draw upon the experiences of others. I would have to assemble my own hard data. However interesting personal and anecdotal experience may be, there is no substitute for the gathering of hard data. Only on the basis of such evidence can one begin to make generalizations regarding the use and abuse of power in church life. If I wanted hard data, I would have to obtain it at first hand; hence the 'power survey' which underlies the following chapters.

Chapter Two

Power in Today's Church: Gathering the Data

1. Responses to the survey proposal

In the summer of 1995 I sent letters to a number of academics seeking their advice on how I might go about gaining the hard data I needed for my research. I wrote:

> The longer I am in ministry the more convinced I am that time and again local churches (as indeed Christian institutions!) are engaged in power struggles. On the one hand, there are ministers who are abusing their power, whether in the way in which they exercise leadership within the congregation as a whole, or in the way in which they abuse trust in terms of their relationships with children and/or members of the opposite sex. On the other hand, many ministers are abused by their congregations – hence the increasing number of enforced terminations of ministry in the Free Churches. However, it is not just a matter of ministers v congregations. Local churches are made up of diverse power groups – for example, deacons on the one hand, and AAEOLs (Angry Alienated Ex-Old Leaders) on the other hand – as also of individual power-brokers.
>
> I believe that there is room for a major contribution in this area. As far as I am aware, very little in this country has been written on the subject of power within the church.
>
> In the absence of any hard data I am proposing to conduct a survey of ministers and other representative 'lay' church leaders on the basis of a detailed questionnaire. In this survey I hope to take a

wide-ranging look at the use and abuse of power in local church life by examining the attitudes of both ministers and churches toward the use of power. I intend to probe such areas as ministerial ambition, the understandings and expectations in ministry with corresponding understandings of success and failure, personality and leadership styles, the relationship between power and authority, structures of power and authority, structures of accountability, the process of change, the handling of conflict and conflict resolution, the degree of honesty and openness in relationships, and the abuses of power by ministers and churches.

Although some years ago I did a survey of 350 English Baptist churches testing out some American hypotheses relating to church growth, I am conscious that on this occasion I would be dealing not so much with 'facts' as with 'attitudes'. This in turn would therefore necessitate a good deal of care in framing the right questions.

It is at this point that I would seek your advice. First of all, are there issues you feel I would need to look at which I do not appear to have thought of? Indeed, are there books and/or articles which you feel I should read at this early stage? Secondly, is there any competent sociologist you could point me to, who is used to drafting questionnaires and who would be sympathetic to the area I propose to investigate? Clearly some understanding of church life would be necessary. Thirdly, would you be aware of any funds into which I might be able to tap to cover some of the costs involved in this project?

Most of the replies were encouraging, insofar as all acknowledged that here was an area of interest and of concern. For example, one principal of a theological college wrote: 'Recent conversations . . . suggest to me that there is an urgent need to explore the issue further.' 'The project . . . sounds an intriguing one', replied a Cambridge don.

A senior academic whose expertise includes the sociology of religion likewise strongly supported my engaging in this area of proposed research: 'The questions you raise are very crucial ones for churches – and yet seldom discussed for obvious reasons. I suspect that as churchgoing continues to decline in Britain so some of the more dysfunctional sides of those few who do still go to church will become more apparent. A rather depressing thought

. . . I am sure that research in this area should be done, but I suspect that many churches will be very suspicious of it.'

A distinguished American church growth consultant replied at some length:

> I can only be supportive of any efforts you would make about dishonest uses and abuses of power within congregational systems. Within the past ten days I have been privileged to be a consultant within two larger congregational systems, where power was clearly being abused. The brunt of the abuse was the senior pastor.
>
> The first was a Jewish synagogue . . . where I spent a week covering and dehumanizing the thrust of power. Both the senior Rabbi and his associate had been in the congregation about ten years. At this juncture in their history, the persons in power positions on the executive committee of their Board of Trustees decided they had a distinct liking for the associate Rabbi and a distinct dislike for the senior Rabbi. To be sure, the senior Rabbi is not without fault, and has certainly shot himself in the foot and during some very key times. Nonetheless, I found him to be a very talented, capable and committed Rabbi. It is my sense of things, that had I not intervened in this week, that he would have been out of there within six months. Even with this timely intervention, it is touch and go whether he will be able to sustain his ministry in that place.
>
> Similarly, I was involved for two days in a large Lutheran congregation . . . This situation also involved a capable senior and associate pastor. The associate, being female, was placing some clear pressure on the senior pastor, wanting more elbow room for an expanded ministry. The senior pastor, male, had just endured a series of crises in his personal life. I believe this caused him to be quite scattered, resulting in some key mistakes he made in his ministry related to last minute efforts he made in trying to press forward some of his agenda. Once again, the executive committee of the board, a group of highly capable business administrators, found themselves dealing with this situation by moving into the pastor's territory and actually assuming responsibility for some of the day-to-day operations of the congregation. As a group of power people, they clearly intimidated the senior pastor, who felt himself back down, one side from the female associate and from the other side to an aggressive administrative board. I discovered that the whole church council were also miffed at the way in which the

executive council had moved in and made decisions on behalf of the congregation, squeezing out the pastor. Also the church council members would not admit that there was a power struggle going on between the senior pastor and the executive committee. All this was having a great emotional impact on the pastor, who was acting out in even more strange ways.

I believe it goes without saying that whenever you have more than three people in some kind of intentional community, you are going to have a political community, hence, power dynamics. I hope your research and book would acknowledge this, then take it a step further to the clear abuses that can take place within religious systems. I would concur that there are some clergy who simply through the power of their persona and their position abuse lay people.

Unfortunately, little help was available from most of those to whom I had written. Certainly no money was on offer!

2. The involvement of Linda Jones and Partners

At this point I encountered a piece of good fortune. One of my church members indicated that he was willing and interested in assisting me in my research. This offer proved to be of crucial importance. Although Bert Thrift had no academic expertise in the area of my proposed research, he is a qualified statistician, a Member of the Market Research Society, who for many years ran a highly successful market research business. Being semi-retired, he had time to offer. He was an ideal person to help set the project on a scientific basis.

As I shared my ideas and my enthusiasm, Bert realized that further help was needed. This was given by his daughter-in-law, Linda Jones, whose independent market research firm – Linda Jones and Partners of Orford, near Woodbridge, Suffolk – is registered by the Market Research Society.

As I mentioned in my letter of enquiry, over 25 years ago I was involved, together with Alan Wilkinson, then Administrator of the Manchester Business School, in a major questionnaire-based survey of over 350 English Baptist Churches, intended to test some American hypotheses about church growth.[1] Although in many ways a most complicated exercise, in which we had used what was then the largest computer in the North West of England to gather together a vast amount of statistical information, this church growth research now seemed relatively straightforward compared to the new project. Alan Wilkinson and I had been dealing primarily with numbers, whereas the research into power involved attitudes.

Is it possible to conduct an investigation of people's attitudes on the basis of a questionnaire-based survey? Bert Thrift and Linda Jones believed it was and with their encouragement I produced a long list of questions which they turned into a professional questionnaire.

3. The pilot survey

Before being circulated, it was tested by means of a pilot survey in the autumn of 1995. This involved five ministers – two young Anglicans, and three senior Free Church ministers – two Baptists and one Methodist. (A URC minister withdrew because of the pressure of his other commitments.) Each minister was sent the draft questionnaire, following which Linda conducted an in-depth interview with each minister.

The results of the survey were very encouraging. Linda Jones reported:

> All respondents seem to be in agreement that power is a problem in the church, and can cite many examples of themselves being at the receiving end of power abuse, either from the congregation, the deacons/officials or indeed the hierarchy above them.
> What they are less able to recognize is their own abuses of power. Some appreciate that they have probably overstepped the mark in the

---

[1] This was later written up and published by the Bible Society in 1980 as *Turning the Tide: An assessment of Baptist Church Growth in England*.

past, but feel they can justify this as it was for 'the good of the church' rather than their own personal ends. Others feel that their church needs a strong leader, and as such it is more difficult to draw the line between where leadership ends and power begins.

On the basis of this pilot survey the questionnaire was revised. In particular we sought to sharpen up some of the questions to help respondents recognize and confront issues. In the process of redrafting and revising we found ourselves adding further questions, but decided to remove others. It was not an easy task: we would have liked to have asked twice, if not three times, as many questions as there were in the final listing. We were constrained not only by the cost of printing and postage but perhaps even more by the probability that the longer the questionnaire, the less likely people would be to fill it in and return it.

All this took time – not least because we all had other commitments – so it was not until the Spring of 1996 that we were in a position to send out the revised questionnaire.

4. The Richard Baxter Institute for Ministry

Ideally the questionnaire would have been sent to every minister in every denomination. But where would the funds have come from? We decided to take as a sample the mailing list of the Richard Baxter Institute for Ministry (RBIM).[2]

---

2 Richard Baxter, from whom the RBIM draws its inspiration, exercised a notable ministry in Kidderminster during the Civil War and the Restoration. He is best known for his book, *The Reformed Pastor*, which although published in 1656, remains a classic textbook for Christian ministry. In his case 'reformed' was not a theological label; Baxter's sympathies were broad and he was above all concerned for spiritual 'renewal'. He wrote: 'All churches either rise or fall as the ministry doth rise or fall – not in riches or worldly grandeur, but in knowledge, zeal, and ability for their work.' In more modern language: 'The key to the health and growth of the churches is its leaders.'

The RBIM, founded in 1995, is an interdenominational organization with members from all the non-Roman mainline denominations. Its aim is 'to promote excellence in the practice of ministry, enabling ministers and pastoral leaders to become increasingly effective in the mission to which Christ has called them'. In addition to holding regular day conferences, it also publishes a journal, entitled *Ministry Today*, in conjunction with the Bible Society, three times a year.[3]

As Chairman of the RBIM I asked the Board of Trustees for permission to use the mailing list. Although there was some danger of bias in using such a self-selecting sample, we felt that RBIM members, as ministers interested in the practise of ministry, might perhaps be more likely to be open and self-aware than others, and might be more willing to complete and return the questionnaires.

4.1 Confidentiality

If respondents were to be open in their replies, confidentiality needed to be guaranteed. The survey was therefore formally commissioned by the RBIM Board of Trustees and carried out by Linda Jones and Partners. Although I had originally commissioned the survey, I would see none of the returned questionnaires but only the statistical data as presented to me by Linda Jones and Partners. Linda was accordingly able to write in the letter which accompanied the questionnaires:

> We have been commissioned by the Richard Baxter Institute for Ministry to conduct a survey on leadership styles in the local church. . . .
> The immediate purpose of this research is to examine how ministers exercise leadership in their churches, and in particular to explore how they handle issues such as conflict and power in their day-to-day church life. Through theological reflection on the data gained, the

---

[3] Further information about the Richard Baxter Institute for Ministry can be obtained from the membership secretary, Mrs Mary Watson, 82 Watchouse Lane, Chelmsford, Essex.

intention is then to develop models for the use of power and authority which are rooted in the Biblical pattern for the people of God living their life together. In other words, the overall objective of this project is essentially practical and hopefully will benefit both churches and leaders, enabling them to engage more effectively in their ministry and mission. We anticipate the results of the research will eventually be published – in the first place in *Ministry Today*, but also possibly in book form.

We believe this to be a very valuable survey and would greatly appreciate your co-operation. Can we assure you that your answers will be treated in strictest confidence, in accordance with the Market Research Society's Code of Conduct. This means that no information that could identify you will be passed on to the commissioner of the survey – only the results of the survey as a whole.

4.2 The sample

The sample mailed comprised 231 ministers in pastoral charge who were members of the RBIM. But realizing that the sample might be considered somewhat small, we also included a further ministerial questionnaire in the mailing, in the hope that RBIM members might be willing to pass them on to a ministerial colleague. In addition, because we believed it was not sufficient to obtain the views of ministers only, we also sent similar questionnaires to be filled in by two representative 'lay' leaders of the minister's choosing (e.g. church warden, church secretary, church treasurer, etc.).

Each of the 231 ministers comprising the initial sample were sent a package consisting of three envelopes containing:

Envelope I: Letter of explanation, the questionnaire, and a stamped addressed return envelope.

Envelope II: A second explanatory letter, two questionnaires (each with its own stamped addressed return envelope) to pass on to two of the officers in their church. These questionnaires were similar to the main questionnaire, but amended where necessary.

Envelope III: A further set of the material contained in Envelope I, for the ministerial members of the RBIM to pass on to a colleague in another church in their area.

The questionnaires were sent out on 27 March 1996, and reminders were sent to non-respondent RBIM members on 18 April and 9 May. The survey was closed at the end of May 1996.

4.3 Response

Of the 231 ministers who were members of the RBIM, 116 (50% of the sample) returned a questionnaire in full.

(A further 35 members of the RBIM – 15% of the sample – replied without completing the questionnaire. Of these ministers, 6 simply returned the blank questionnaire. The other 29 gave various reasons for non-completion: lack of time [14]; dislike of some of the questions [7]; illness [3]; another minister in the church had returned a questionnaire [2]; only been at church a short time [2]; retired [1].)

In other words, of the 231 ministers in the RBIM sample, 151 (65%) responded in one way or another – a good response, when compared with other questionnaire-based postal surveys.

Additional responses came from a further 25 ministers, not members of the RBIM, bringing the total sample of ministers in the survey up to 141.

Of the church officials, 120 replied. However, since we excluded from the survey officials whose minister had not responded, the final sample figure for church officials was 112.

4.4 The data gained

Before examining the data, two points need to be made clear. First, that although the vast majority of respondents completed the questionnaire in great detail, there were inevitably some who did not answer every question. This explains why the percentages do not quite add up to 100%. Second, although I am responsible for the interpretation of the data, the market research professionals have made certain that I have not misinterpreted the data provided.

Copies of the two questionnaires are to be found in the appendices to this book.

Chapter Three

Power Grid – Analysing the Context

A grid may be defined as a supportive framework. In this chapter we shall examine in detail the framework of church life within which 'power games' are played. The 'power games' themselves are treated in Chapter Four. Some of the analysis is admittedly not immediately relevant to our theme. Nonetheless, in view of the dearth of hard data about ministry in general, material has been included which is of more general interest for ministry. However, the general focus remains on the issue of power.

1. Classification data

At the outset, both questionnaires sought to gain some basic information regarding both the respondents and their churches.

1.1 The church

Denomination

Baptist churches	40%
Anglican	20%
URC/Congregational	20%
Methodist	8%
'Independents'	3%
'Other'	9%

In denominational terms this is not a representative survey. To a very large extent it focuses on the Free Churches – not surprisingly since the Richard Baxter Institute for Ministry had its initial roots in Baptist church life. Yet in the UK there are more Anglican clergy (13,543) than Free Church (11,251). In addition some 9,000 Roman Catholic clergy are not represented at all.[1]

Size of church

Up to 150 people at Sunday service	67%
Over 150 people at Sunday service	32%

Because of our limited statistical base, we have found it convenient to use 150 as the cut-off point to distinguish between smaller and larger churches. We accept that in a wider context this distinction may be somewhat misleading. In a British context, for instance, a small church is normally classed as a church with a Sunday congregation of less than 50. In England some 36% of all churches have a weekly adult attendance of 50 or less.

Number of churches

Ministers with pastoral oversight of one church only	65%
Pastoral oversight of two churches	16%
Pastoral oversight of three churches	6%
Pastoral oversight of four churches	6%
Pastoral oversight of 5 churches or more	4%

Most ministers had pastoral oversight of a single church, but more than a quarter (26%) had oversight of two churches or more.

Social class

Churches of mainly working-class people	18%
Churches of mainly academic/professional people	33%
Churches equally divided between the two above	47%

---

1 *UK Christian Handbook* 1996/1997 edition (Christian Research, London SE9 2TZ) 240.

The American church growth specialist, Peter Wagner, maintains that working-class congregations mostly prefer strong leadership. We were not able to test this hypothesis.

We were able to test the occupation of the church officials. On the basis of an analysis of their returns, the church officials fitted into the following socio-economic groupings:

Church officials: socio-economic groups

Class A	8%
Class B	26%
Class C1	23%
Class C2	3%
Class D	4%
Class E	4%

32% of church officials gave no information on this point: age analysis suggests this would largely have been because the respondents had retired. Nonetheless on the basis of the returns we can say that on socio-economic grounds the church officials did not exactly match their churches. Probably ministers tend to be more representative of their congregations, if the *Sunday Times* is right in describing the clergy as 'middle-class men living in upper-class houses on a working-class income'.[2] On the other hand, the formal theological college education received by the vast majority of ministers probably alienates from the working class even those ministers who had similar roots.

Theological position

The theological position of the churches varied, although the majority were clearly in the evangelical tradition. Such a response is unrepresentative of British churches in general. The Evangelical Alliance, for instance, reckons to speak on behalf of only some 4,000 churches.[3] The preponderance of evangelical churches in

---

[2] *Sunday Times*, 25 November 1984.
[3] Strictly speaking, as at June 1996, only 2887 individual churches are in membership with the Evangelical Alliance.

this survey therefore betrays the roots of the Richard Baxter Institute for Ministry.

The responses were a little confusing since respondents were allowed to tick more than one box; in addition some were responsible for more than one church. The responses were as follows:

Theological position

Evangelical	75%
Middle of the road	40%
Charismatic	33%
Liberal	12%
Fundamentalist	6%
Catholic	2%

The minister

Sex

Men	97%
Women	3%

The vast majority of ministers were male – in line with the in-built male bias still present in ordained Christian ministry.

It would be an interesting exercise to compare the way in which women handle the power issue in comparison with men. There seems to be a tendency for women to be much more perceptive than men and often able to exercise their ministry much more effectively than many men. They are also better at making and developing relationships. Lyle Schaller maintains that 'women pastors make changes faster with less resistance; they are generally over-achievers and nurturers; men don't easily say to a woman "that's a dumb idea" '.[4]

---

4 Unfortunately I have not been able to find the original source of this remark.

Age

Ministers under 45   45%

Ministers over 45   45%

Although an earlier survey had revealed that churches with ministers aged 30–39 showed a strong bias toward growth,[5] in this present study age did not seem to be a very significant factor. Being myself in my fifties, I would like to believe that age brings wisdom. On the other hand, age does not inevitably bring increased wisdom. For learning to take place, there must be a good deal of personal reflection. A cause of concern is that reflection on ministerial practice, as also in-service training, tend to be optional extras taken up by only a minority of ministers. Whereas in most professions today in-service training is a necessity, most ministers are not engaged in updating their personal and professional skills. In addition, where continuing education does occur, it often revolves around the traditional theological disciplines. It follows that in this respect one can learn very little from a minister's age. Older ministers inevitably are more experienced, but how much they may have learnt from their experience may sometimes be open to question. Younger ministers inevitably have more energy, but whether the energy is always rightly channelled may be equally open to question.

Marital status

Married   96%

Single   2%

Divorced   1%

Widowed   0

Although an increasing proportion of the population is divorced, this is not reflected in ministry. In one sense this is commendable. One would not want ministers to reflect the national divorce statistics. On the other hand, does this sample contain an unduly

---

[5] Paul Beasley-Murray & Alan Wilkinson, *Turning the Tide* 32.

low percentage of the divorced or separated in ministry?[6] Perhaps this in part reflects the theological bias of the churches in the survey.

As far as single clergy are concerned, in the more evangelical churches, if not generally, there tends to be a bias against the unmarried, and in particular against single men. When seeking a minister, most churches want a married man with 2.4 children. Single women are by and large acceptable. Sadly the sexuality of single men is often regarded with suspicion. What amounts to a 'dearth' of single ministers means that ministry – and therefore its emphases – is quite unrepresentative of Britain as a whole, where out of some 46 million nearly 17 million – over one-third (36%) – are single. In fact, the ministry is in this respect unrepresentative of the church. The Evangelical Alliance found that about 35% of adults in churches were single; only a little less than the national figure for the whole population.[7]

Spouses

Spouses having a regular paid job	49%
Spouses without a regular paid job	46%

As one might expect, for age 45+ this figure rose to 54% at work, and 43% not at work.

By comparison with the rest of the population, the proportion of those not at work is fairly high. Is there still pressure in some churches for the minister's wife to fulfil the role of an unpaid curate? The survey would suggest that this could be so. For

---

[6] There appear to be no overall national statistics with regard to the breakdown of clergy marriages. Mary Kirk and Tom Leary in *Holy Matrimony? An Exploration of Marriage and Ministry* (Lynx, Oxford 1994)13-16 suggest that clergy marital breakdown is very much on the increase. The quote Pam Dawson, secretary of Broken Rites, the association for divorced and separated clery wives, who said that in their first year (1983) they had twenty-eight inquiries, building up to around fifty per year.

[7] *Belonging: A Resource for the Christian Family* (Baptist Union, Didcot 1994) 42.

example 46% reported that their wife had a recognized role in the church. The role varied enormously.

Church role of wife

Leader of toddler or pre-school group	6%
Sunday School teacher / youth leader	6%
Secretary or administrator	4%
Member of singing or music group	4%
Leader of a women's group	2%
'Other'	17%

The figure of 2% leading a women's group certainly stands on its head the traditional picture of the minister's wife!

Finance and spouses

In spite of the Apostle Paul's teaching that 'leaders should be considered worthy of receiving double pay, especially those who work hard at preaching and teaching' (1 Tim. 3:17 GNB), the financial rewards of ministry are limited: 36% of ministers in the survey earned less than £12,500 p.a., and only 12% earned over £15,000. Only one minister earned more than £20,000 – and he was a Baptist! The general salary figures should probably be adjusted upwards by £2,500 or more, since 74% of ministers live in rent-free accommodation; nonethless the resulting figures are certainly not over-generous.

Although the question of financial remuneration was not developed, this is a real issue for many ministers – and their spouses. Traditionally ministers receive a 'stipend' rather than a 'salary' – the distinction being that a 'stipend' is an 'allowance' providing sufficient money for the needs of a minister, as distinct from giving a 'reward' for services rendered. This distinction may well be fair if it simply concerns a single person, but what if it involves a family too? To what extent is it fair or right to expect the minister's family to share in the ministerial calling? It has not been unknown for ministers to be told that they should set an example of 'holy poverty' – but should this include families too?

The issue of financial remuneration becomes even more acute in churches where the minister's salary is fixed not by some central body, but by the local church itself. For many ministers and their spouses this creates a real sense of powerlessness, insofar as their welfare is being decided by others – there is normally nobody with a specific brief to represent their interests in the church's discussion. Time and again the discussion revolves around what the church feels it can afford to pay, rather than what might be fair and just.

Linked with the issue of salary is also the issue of housing. Traditionally ministers have been expected to live in tied accommodation, whether it be a manse or vicarage. However, many ministers – and particularly spouses – resent this provision. They do not wish to be dependent upon the church. Indeed, this dependency creates within them a sense of unwished-for 'powerlessness'.[8]

Such a situation might have been expected to act as a strong financial incentive for wives to go out to work, let alone to fulfil themselves in a career of one kind or another. But in fact, just under half (49%) of all spouses in the survey had a regular paid job. The percentages changed a little when account was taken of age: 54% of spouses over 45 had a paid job as against 41% of those under 45.

Length of time in ministry and in present church
In ministry for more than 15 years	45%
In their present church for more than five years	46%

Since entrants to ministry no longer tend to be in their early twenties, the first figure is probably 'par for the course' in a survey where 55% are over forty-five.

For any pastors worth their salt, such pastoral longevity should certainly consolidate their position ('power') in the church. For the longer ministers are involved in people's lives, the more opportunity there is for bonds of love and affection to

---

[8] See Alistair Ross, *Evangelicals in Exile* (Darton, Longman & Todd, London 1997) 133.

be developed and strengthened. The more pastors are perceived to love and care for their people, the greater is their authority. Such authority ('power') by definition cannot be present in the opening chapter of a pastor's ministry.

As an aside we may note that in church growth terms pastoral longevity is also a good sign, for as the earlier survey confirmed, a bias toward growth tends to appear only after a minister has been some five years in a church.[9]

British ministers tend to stay longer in their churches than their American cousins. In the Southern Baptist Convention of the USA, for example, pastors move on the average of every 18–20 months. In part this is because of the large number of 'bi-vocational' ministers in rural areas, who carry on a full-time job along with their pastoral work. However, the tendency may also be due in part to the fact that so many Southern Baptist pastors seem to get either 'pushed out' or 'fired'. In 1985 it was reported that every month 116 Southern Baptist churches sever relationships through involuntary termination. Yet it is not just Southern Baptists who change churches fairly frequently. George Barna reports that during the past decade the average tenure of senior American pastors has dropped from seven to about four years: he attributes this to 'the numbers-crazed, upwardly mobile mentality that plagues the pastorate'.[10]

In both North America and in Britain a pastorate of over ten years is normally regarded as long-term. In this survey 16% fell into that category. Interestingly, of their predecessors, 27% had ministered for over ten years in the church currently in question, with 33% having ministered for some six to ten years.

Duration of interregnum

Under one year	45%
One to two years	17%
Over two years	12%

---

[9] *Turning the Tide* 33,34.
[10] George Barna, *Today's Pastors* (Regal, Ventura, California 1993) 36,37.

Since a large percentage did not reply to the question relating to length of interregnum between themselves and their predecessors, it is difficult to know how much significance to attach to the answers of those who did reply. As a rule of thumb it is often said that the interregnum should be as many months long as the years of the previous ministry. The fact is that churches need sufficient time to 'grieve' before they appoint a successor. This can be particularly true where the previous ministry was of substantial length (e.g. 15 years or more). If that time is not given, then it may not be easy for the new minister to capture the affection of his or her new congregation, particularly where the predecessor was much loved.

Security of tenure

3 months notice	16%
6 months notice	11%
9 months notice	23%
12 months notice	4%
Unspecified	23%
Freehold	18% (mainly Anglican)

In comparison with most jobs, ministers would appear to be very fortunate in respect of security of tenure. On the other hand, in the sight of the law all ministers are self-employed and therefore cannot claim against the church for unfair dismissal. Further, although the number of unemployed ministers is not large, the process of gaining a new 'job' is generally speaking much slower in the ministry than in the secular world. This is due in part to the fact that in most churches the whole church is involved in some aspect of the 'selection' – among Baptists, for instance, it currently takes most ministers a year to move. Furthermore, by comparison with the secular world, gaining a new church almost always involves a geographical move. This in turn involves a considerable upheaval for the family. By contrast, most church members do not work in tied accommodation. If they change jobs, it is often possible for them to remain in the same house. Furthermore, whilst not underestimating the emotional wrench sometimes experienced when members leave a church as a result of a power struggle, their lives, unlike those of ministers and their families, are not turned upside down as a result of the change of church.

What this means is that if there is a power struggle within a church, the minister is in a much weaker position than is sometimes assumed.

Alone or with others?

Exercising a solo ministry	62%
Senior minister with at least one other colleague	25%
Assistant/associate/curate	9%

Although in the Anglican church there is an increasing tendency – in some dioceses at least – for clergy to work in teams, most ministers still work on their own. This is one of the increasing peculiarities of ministry. Few people outside the church work on their own. Whereas in the past certain 'professional' people used to run a one-person practice (e.g. doctors, dentists, accountants) this is much less the case today. Ministry, as we shall see again later, is a very lonely profession.

Where power struggles take place, this form of isolation can often militate against the minister. As the one paid member of staff, the minister can be very vulnerable.

The solo nature of ministry is further underlined by the fact that only 29% of ministers had the services of a full- or part-time church administrator. One might have thought that this 29% more or less equated to the 31% who had over 200 people at worship on a Sunday, but further investigation revealed that this was not the case. Only some 60% of larger churches had a church administrator – as compared to some 20% of smaller churches. Interestingly, of the five largest churches, with congregations of 400–500, three had a church administrator, while two did not.

It would appear that in most churches church administrator is a part-time appointment, for only 13% listed an administrator or a secretary as a member of their church staff. Indeed, if one combines caretakers (9%) with cleaners (8%) who are regarded as members of church staff, then the statistics would indicate that churches tend to put more emphasis on cleanliness rather than efficiency. This lack of professionalism is probably evidenced in the fact that 74% of ministers usually work from home as distinct from 23% who usually work in a church office (this figure rises to 36% of ministers in larger churches).

Theological agreement
As would be expected, theologically the ministers mostly reflected the theological position of their churches. Again the responses are a little misleading in so far as more than one position could be ticked.

    Theological tendency
Evangelical	57%
Charismatic	20%
'Middle of the road'	17%
Liberal	10%
Catholic	4%
Fundamentalist	1%

On the broader question of values, 6% said that they totally shared common values, 88% 'for the most part', and only 5% felt that they did not fit at all.

1.3 Church officials

    Categories of officials
Church secretaries	35%
Church wardens	31%
Church treasurers	22%

Although men predominated (62%), there was a good proportion of women (38%) too. The officials tended to be a little older than the ministers: thus only 35% were under forty-five, 30% were between forty-five and fifty-four, while 33% were over fifty-five. A good deal of experience was represented by these officials:

Years in present church
11–20 years	30%
21–30 years	27%
30+	17%

In terms of Christian service 50% of the church officials had held their present office for more than four years, with 74% having held other offices in the church. Interestingly, as many as 80% of these church officials had belonged to another church, and of these 50% had held office in another church.

Theologically the officials reflected in general the theological position of their ministers.

1.4 Church Growth

A measure of success?

The vast majority of ministers felt that at least to some extent the church measured their success in terms of church growth. Only 19% of ministers felt there was no correlation – a number which reduced to 11% of ministers in churches where over 150 were at Sunday service. However, the number increased to 33% of ministers who regarded themselves as theologically 'middle of the road'.

Certainly in evangelical church circles 'successful' ministries are to a large extent predicated on the ability of a pastor to grow a church. In the past it was sufficient for a pastor to be 'faithful'; today many pastors feel the call is to be 'successful'. This call can prove to be incredibly stressful. Indeed, it is becoming increasingly common for ministers to be asked to leave their churches on the grounds that they are 'not delivering the goods'. The market economy has affected the life of the church as well as the life of the world.

This call to be 'successful' can also be very unfair. Church growth is a complex issue and although ministers have a key role to play, so too do members. If the members are not prepared to move out of the comfort zones of their established patterns of church life, there is very little the minister can do. Likewise the minister is 'powerless' to reverse sociological change, which in turn may have a seriously negative impact upon the life of the church.

Growth patterns

One fascinating detail revealed by the survey is the positive bias toward church growth caused by the arrival of the respondent minister.

Before the arrival of the present minister

Growing strongly	2%
Growing slowly	7%
Holding their own	52%
Declining.	26%

Since the arrival of the respondent minister

Growing strongly	8%
Growing slowly	55%
Holding their own	31%
Declining	6%

Asked about future prospects for growth, 9% thought them excellent, 51% good, 30% fair, and only 5% poor. If these statistics were to be true of the whole country, then the fortunes of the Christian church would have been well and truly reversed.

These replies indicate a very positive frame of mind on the part of the ministers – although it could be argued that this is just another example of ministers feeling pressurized to believe or to state that their churches are growing, since it is something on which they are judged.

This same apparent positive frame of mind was reflected both by ministers who had considered moving out of ministry and by those who had experienced major conflict in ministry.

Ministers are proverbially the worst counters when it comes to telling how many were at church the previous Sunday. As one wag put it, ministers tend to count legs rather than heads! Even if the ministers were accurate in their assessment of increased growth, these figures do not, alas, indicate that their churches have been necessarily any more effective in their mission. There is, for instance, a world of a difference between transfer growth and conversion growth.

2. The Nature of Ministry

2.1 Satisfaction in ministry

Overall there appears to be a good deal of satisfaction in ministry.

Satisfaction in ministry

Very satisfied	29%
Satisfied	57%
Not really satisfied	11%
Not at all satisfied	4%

The degree of satisfaction was underlined by the responses to a further question:

'Has pastoring this church increased your passion for ministry?'

Definitely	40%
To some extent	40%
No	18%*

(*Perhaps significantly this rose to 26% for those over forty-five).

These responses are somewhat surprising. For other research has indicated that a much larger proportion of ministers are either burnt-out or disillusioned. Roy Oswald, admittedly reporting of the American scene, wrote:

> 17% – one out of five – clergy are burned out. This does not imply that they are inactive in parish ministry. They are still able to perform their pastoral functions with skill and concern. The difficulty is that they have lost their zest and enthusiasm for ministry.[11]

---

[11] Roy Oswald, *Clergy Burnout* (Alban Institute, Bethesda 1982) 12.

Within a British context, H.A. Eadie reported that in his survey of 85 Scottish ministers, 68.2% had experienced psychiatric disorders, neurotic problems, personality difficulties and emotional stress of sufficient intensity to require absence from work.[12]

On reflection, this may well be one more instance of where our particular sample of ministers is biased. On the whole, one would not expect burnt-out or disillusioned ministers to be members of the Richard Baxter Institute for Ministry. RBIM members tend to be the enthusiasts for ministry.

Tempted to move out of ministry?

For many clergy in our sample, ministry has not entirely been a bed of roses. 44% said that they had thought of moving out of ministry. This is a large number: over four out of ten ministers have considered giving up. Significantly this 44% is not made up just of the 'dissatisfied' category: 40% of those who declared themselves satisfied had considered moving out of ministry.

Equally significant is that the proportion of ministers who have considered leaving ministry moves up to 59% of ministers under forty-five. This is highly disturbing. The pressures of ministry appear to be increasing.

Various reasons were given for considering moving out of ministry:

The chief cause appeared to be power struggles of one kind or another. Ministers spoke of 'church politics and power', 'wrangles', 'struggles', 'difficulties', 'problems', 'conflict with the leadership', 'a major split', 'the pain inflicted by Christians', 'open hostility especially as a woman', 'total resistance to change, however small, however gentle'.

Associated with such power struggles, another reason frequently given was 'frustration', and the inability to get anywhere. Comments included 'not making much worthwhile headway in congregation', 'feeling ineffective', 'despair', 'sense of failure', 'lethargy of members of the church at times', 'tears'.

---

[12] H.A. Eadie, 'Health of Scottish Clergymen', *Contact* (Winter 1972) 41.

A third factor constantly mentioned was the 'pressure' of pastoral ministry, described in such expressions as 'the holy rat race', 'pressure on family life', 'high expectations', 'pressure to perform'. Several mentioned 'long hours' having to be worked.

Another major factor, although not mentioned quite as often as the three issues of power struggles, frustration and pressure, was finance. One minister spoke of 'having to draw social benefit'. Another wrote: 'I will be leaving the church on 28th April. The church cannot and will not afford my stipend.'

Not surprisingly several referred to disillusionment, whether 'with Christians in the church' or 'with the institutional structures of the church'.

A number mentioned having suffered from depression and burnout.

A few referred to 'the grind of administration'; '. . . ministry is now management/paper-pushing and I've no managerial training.'

Interestingly only one person said he had considered leaving ministry due to 'some questioning of basic faith'. In this survey at least, ministers do not appear to be experiencing crises of faith – or if they are, then they did not feel able to acknowledge the crisis.

Of those who said they had never thought of moving out of ministry, the overwhelming majority attributed their remaining in ministry to the call of God, as a result of which they felt they had no choice. 'Ministry is my life calling'; 'I feel I am doing what God has called me to do'; 'I believe it's where the Lord wants me to be.'

Some also mentioned job satisfaction and a sense of the 'worthwhile nature' of what they were doing. 'Fulfilment'; 'No other work is so privileged and rich in human/divine activity.' Others felt that in this ministerial role they could best use their gifts and serve God. One respondent spoke of the 'freedom and variety' encountered in ministry; another of the 'opportunities' for ministry. Yet another referred to 'the challenge of meeting such a diverse group of people, and doing this in the name of Christ'. 'It is what I want to do.'

The only discordant note came from the minister who wrote: 'Not otherwise qualified and do not have another house or sufficient money to buy one'. Actually, there is a good deal of generalized truth in this remark. There was a time, for instance, when it was relatively easy for ministers to move into teaching or into social work. But the job-market has changed. Ministers increasingly feel themselves powerless to find another job. The result is that some remain in ministry for the sake of their monthly pay-packet. They have lost their sense of call as also their motivation for ministry – and yet they feel themselves trapped. The fact that this phenomenon was not revealed in this survey is probably due to the bias of the sample – members of RBIM tend to be motivated ministers.

2.2 Ministry and the family

'Has pastoring this church has been difficult on your family?'

Definitely	23%*
To some extent	49%
No	26%

*Rising to 33% of those in larger churches

It would have been interesting if ministers' wives had answered this question – the likelihood is that the figures would have been higher. The fact is that the pressures faced by most ministerial families are considerably higher than other domestic set-ups. The phenomenon, for instance, of having to live in a kind of goldfish bowl, where the life of the pastor and of the pastor's family is continually on display, can be highly stressful. Although admittedly some of the stresses can be self-imposed, they can also be imposed by the church too.

One Anglican bishop listed the following factors which combine to distinguish clergy families from others:

- tied housing and fixed-term appointments
- few resources
- moral standards
- public image to keep up

- expectations of ideal family
- ill-defined boundaries between work and home life
- doing the Lord's work – spouses compete with God
- coyness about using counselling agencies when difficulties occur.[13]

It is interesting to compare the responses of our survey with Barna's survey of American pastors. In his survey to precisely the same question Barna received the following answers:

(Has pastoring this church has been difficult on your family? – USA)

Very true	11%
Somewhat true	38%
Not too true	33%
Not at all true	8%.

While in the American survey one out of ten admitted that their family had suffered greatly as a result of current church ministry,[14] the proportion is much higher in our British survey. This is a cause for concern. The damage being done to ministers' children is considerable. Here is a form of power abuse on the part of the church, no doubt unintentional, which can have devastating results.

2.3 Ministry and ambition

Would you hope to move on to a larger church?

Definitely	11%
To some extent	23%
No	58%

The reason for not wanting to move on to a larger church may be that most of them (49% of the total number of ministers) did not feel they could accomplish more in another church.

---

[13] Cited in Kirk & Leary, *Holy Matrimony?* 39,40.
[14] Barna, *Today's Pastors* 61-63.

Age did not appear significant. Indeed, of those under forty-five only 8% said they 'definitely' hoped to move on to a larger church, although some 37% said that they hoped 'to some extent'.

Where a difference did emerge was in cases where ministers had classed themselves as being 'not very' or 'not at all' powerful. 76% of these less powerful ministers said that they did not want to move on to a larger church. Correspondingly, of those who thought of themselves as 'very' or 'moderately' powerful as people, 15% said they 'definitely' wanted to move to a larger church, and 28% said 'to some extent'. Overall, however, the drive to move on to bigger and better churches does not seem to be so widespread as some have appeared to suggest.

'Do you feel you could accomplish more in another church?'

Definitely	12%
To some extent	32%
No	49%

The only significant variation was amongst those who said they were enjoying their current ministry 'quite a lot': 14% said they definitely could accomplish more elsewhere and 41% to some extent, with only 39% saying 'No'.

Not surprisingly, of those who were enjoying ministry 'a lot', only 6% said they definitely could accomplish more elsewhere, with another 25% saying 'to some extent': 61% of them felt they could not accomplish more.

Overall most ministers feel that they are being fulfilled in their present church. This is surely a good sign and might be understood as meaning that God has truly called them to their present place of service!

Yet in spite of that sense of fulfilment only 32% felt their gifts were being fully used in their present church. This surely is a cause for concern, even though a further 49% felt their gifts were being used to some extent. One wonders if these ministers have ever shared their frustration with their churches. Is it significant that of those ministers who described themselves as 'charismatic' 46% said they felt their gifts were being fully used in the church? The only group to score higher was composed of those enjoying ministry a lot: 51% said they felt their gifts were definitely being fully used, with a further 41% saying 'to some extent'.

Even though most ministers did not want to move on to a larger church, only 10% felt they lacked the capacity to pastor a bigger church. On average, 48% believed they definitely had the necessary gifts, with a further 34% believing 'to some extent'. Not surprisingly the differences were particularly evident between those who categorized themselves as 'very' or 'moderately' powerful people and those who saw themselves as 'not very' or 'not at all' powerful people: 58% of the former believed they definitely had the capacity over against 24% of the latter; while only 6% of the former said they did not believe they had the capacity. Overall, rightly or wrongly, most ministers seem to have a fairly good opinion of their capabilities.

The majority of ministers (60%) said that they would not like – or have liked – to be a bishop-figure. There was a clear difference, however, between smaller and larger churches. 68% of ministers in smaller churches said 'No' compared to only 44% of ministers in larger churches. Of those ministering in larger churches 13% said they would definitely like (or have liked) such ecclesiastical preferment, with another 33% saying they would like (or have liked) such preferment 'to some extent'. Overall, most ministers did not seem interested in ecclesiastical preferment. Indeed, of those under forty-five only 6% said they were definitely interested: for the rest there seemed to be little allure in any power or prestige which might belong to an episcopal office. Maybe in comparison with day-to-day life such positions seemed – and probably are – dull and unattractive.

Does all this mean, therefore, that ministers are not generally ambitious? Robert Schnase, a Methodist minister working in Texas, claims that

> Most pastors would not want their peers to describe them as ambitious. They might appreciate being called energetic, hard-working, effective, or competent, but ambitious stirrings are downplayed, forbidden, hidden from public view. On the other hand, most pastors

would not enjoy being described as unambitious. The word brings to mind laziness and ineffectiveness.[15]

In our survey a good number admitted to being ambitious:

Ambition
very ambitious	13%
fairly ambitious	48%
not very ambitious	29%
not at all ambitious.	9%

One or two clearly felt it wrong to be ambitious: 'Ambition should not be relevant in Christian ministry', wrote one. 'Servanthood and ambition are somewhat contradictory.' Another stated: 'I am not interested in the demand for money, numbers and results, now defining 'successful' ministry.'

The two most ambitious groups appeared to be, on the one hand, those who saw themselves as charismatic, and on the other hand the Baptists: 23% of both groups described themselves as very ambitious! As one would expect, the least ambitious were those who described themselves as 'not very' or 'not at all' powerful: 24% said they were not at all ambitious. In general terms, however, the majority of ministers (61%) are ambitious to some degree.

The positives and negatives of ministerial ambition
A significant number of ministers see ambition as having had a positive role in their ministry:

Ambition: a positive factor?
Very positive	12%
Fairly positive	26%

---

[15] Robert Schnase, *Ambition in Ministry\: Our spiritual struggle with success, achievement and competition* (Abingdon Press, Nashville 1993) 18.

Many examples were given of how ambition had been a positive force for good. A large number centred around the way in which ambition had encouraged 'excellence' and 'higher standards' in ministry with a corresponding desire to be 'the best we can be'.

For others, ambition 'leads to my being stretched and taking initiatives'; 'I want to press on to "greater things.' Several said that ambition has caused them to become more 'imaginative' and to be prepared 'to take risks'.

Ambition leads others to want to become more 'professional', which in turn leads to the seeking of 'training opportunities'.

Some mentioned how ambition has led them to become more 'forward looking' and in turn caused them to 'set achievable, measurable and specific goals'.

Several spoke of how ambition had motivated them to 'work harder'. 'It has been a powerful emotion to motivate study, discipline and professionalism.'

One spoke of how personal ambition had affected the life of the church in general: 'it spreads enthusiasm into the life of the church.'

Very few ministers said they felt ambition had affected their ministry negatively:

Fairly negatively	2%
Very negatively	1%.

On the other hand, when asked to give examples of how ambition had impacted their ministry negatively, a large number of examples was given. There was repeated reference to how ambition caused ministers to become 'driven' and to impose 'unnecessary pressure on self'. Ambition leads to the 'danger of aiming for perfection'; 'creating unrealistic targets and expectations'.

To a large extent ambition appears to be linked with church growth: 'I sometimes push for numbers rather than disciples.' Several spoke of tending to 'measure my effectiveness by numerical growth', with the result that when church growth does not take place they begin to doubt their own effectiveness. Ambition may lead ministers to look for 'a better future rather than seeking God where they are'.

Ministry and competition
Linked with ambition is often a sense of competitiveness.

> *Competitiveness*
> Very competitive   17%
> Competitive   40%
> Not at all competitive   8%

Clearly the majority of ministers are competitive. Ministers in larger churches seemed to be the most competitive: 27% of such ministers said they were very competitive, and 38% said they were quite competitive. Possibly this higher percentage is a partial reflection of the North American scene, of which Darius Salter writes: 'The successful pastor is highly competitive and would rather fight an uphill battle than coast downhill . . . He loves new challenges and does not mind attempting the novel or unusual.'[16]

> *'With whom are you competing?'*
> Did not specify   52%
> With myself   21%
> With ministers in other churches   9%
> With an 'ideal' or 'key value'   9%

Variations on the overall norm were provided by ministers under forty-five, 35% of whom said they were competing with themselves and 12% with ministers in other churches. Furthermore, 13% of ministers in larger churches and 18% of charismatics said they felt they were competing with ministers in other churches.

Personal experience of ministers' fraternals would have led one to anticipate that the figures of those competing with other

---

[16] Darius Salter, *What Really Happens in Ministry* 24.

ministers would have been greatly higher for every group! Envy is generally reckoned to be one of the cardinal sins of ministry. Ministers constantly compare themselves with one another. If this is so, then why did most of those ministers claiming to be competitive fail to say with whom they were competing? Was it because they did not like to own up to this darker side of themselves?

Professional goals

'What professional goals do you have?'
This question was answered in many different ways. Typical of one type of response were: 'None – except to maintain a sense of integrity in ministry and earn my stipend' and 'To remain in pastoral ministry'. Similarly, perhaps, a number spoke of their desire 'to be faithful'.

Many spoke of the development of particular skills and competencies: 'To be a more effective leader, especially in the role of facilitator – getting the best out of others'; 'to improve my preaching and my teaching'; 'to be competent at leading worship, pastoral care and administration'; to be effective in evangelism'; 'to structure time more efficiently'; 'to develop management, communication and counselling skills'.

Some spoke more generally of their desire to grow and reach their full potential. Others wanted more professional training: 'to have a formal professional qualification in counselling and training'. Several said they were possibly interested in gaining a master's degree. One wanted 'to gain a PhD and write more books and articles'.

Several were interested in developing a 'wider ministry' beyond the local church.

On the whole one has to admit that the goals were remarkably unspecific. With a few exceptions, they were far from being measurable in any way, with the result that it would be difficult to know when, if ever, such goals were achieved! Indeed, the ministers who answered that they had no professional goals were probably being more honest than those whose answers appeared to be completely vague. The disturbing overall conclusion to be drawn is that most ministers have neither the ability nor the skill to formalize more concrete goals.

Personal goals

- The personal goals of many had to do with their relationship with God: 'to know God better'; 'to become more like Christ'; 'greater holiness'.
- Very few related their personal goals to any sense of growth and development as a person.
- Many mentioned a desire to 'be a good husband and father': One spoke of his ambition to 'survive teenagers', another of his ambition 'to enjoy my grandchildren'.
- Others wanted to develop more time for their hobbies and leisure activities, whether it be in terms of travelling, driving a racing car, playing the clarinet, or generally keeping fit.
- A few wanted to write: e.g. on gerontology and ecclesiastical history. One wanted to 'write the story of my life and ministry from an anonymous standpoint'.
- Several were looking forward to retirement.
- 'At this stage survival' and 'to remain sane' were, one hopes, tongue in cheek responses. 'To withdraw completely from church life', however, did not sound amusing.
- Perhaps equally sad were those who simply stated: 'None'. They had no personal goals.

Managing Time

Unlike most people, ministers have no set hours of work. Theirs is not a nine to five job. In theory they are on duty twenty-four hours a day. Many ministers are formally entitled to only one day off a week. How they shape their working week is left to them. Some find it incredibly hard to be self-disciplined: hence the notorious number of workaholics in the ranks of the ministry.

Certainly in this survey ministers reckon themselves to be hard-working. On average, ministers reckoned that they worked 64.3 hours per week. When one remembers that this is an average, then clearly some must be working very hard indeed.

A question about the number of hours worked on average in various categories produced the following:

	Hours
Sermon preparation and preaching	7.5
Visiting – building and maintaining meaningful relationships	7.5
Administration	6.5
Prayer and meditation	6.2
Worship preparation and leading worship	5.7
Study	5.6
Committees	5.3
Community involvement and social action	4.3
Discipling and nurturing	4.2
Counselling	4.1
Enabling and involving laity in ministry	4.1
Evangelism	3.3

An enormous amount of time appears to be devoted to the Sunday services, totalling, if one includes preparation and study, almost 19 hours. Maintaining the organizational life of the church (administration and committees) amounts to almost 12 hours. Pastoral care, as represented by counselling and visiting, amounts to 11.6 hours. Mission, i.e. community involvement and evangelism, amounts to 8.6 hours. By contrast, investing in the lives of others, hopefully with a view to their being involved in Christian service (discipling and enabling) occupies just over 8 hours. Is this a right use of a minister's time? Would churches tend to grow more if less time was given to preparing for Sunday services (e.g. by doing away with the evening service)? Would churches benefit if ministers were largely relieved from their administrative and organizational functions, and instead were able to devote more time to helping their members be involved in ministry and mission?

The joys of ministry
Ministers were asked to estimate their 'enjoyment rating' on a scale of 0 – 10. It will be seen that the ratio between hours worked and the 'enjoyment factor' varies considerably.

	Hours	Enjoyment rating
Sermon preparation and preaching	7.5	7.9
Worship preparation and leading worship	5.7	7.5
Discipling and nurturing	4.2	7.5
Study	5.6	7.4
Enabling and involving laity in ministry	4.1	7.2
Prayer and meditation	6.2	7.1
Visiting – building and maintaining meaningful relationships	7.5	7.1
Evangelism	3.3	6.8
Counselling	4.1	6.4
Community involvement and social action	4.3	5.9
Administration	6.5	4.7
Committees	5.3	4.6

The greatest joy of most ministers is preaching and the associated sermon preparation. Study also comes high up the list. They also greatly enjoy discipling/nurturing and leading/preparing for worship, as also their time for prayer and meditation. Visiting/building and maintaining meaningful relationships also scores well.

Problems and frustrations of ministry
Ministers were asked to rate on a score of 0–10 the issues they felt to present major problems or to inflict the greatest frustration.

Issue	Average Rating
How to do effective outreach	6.3
Lack of commitment on part of members	5.9
Low level of spiritual maturity of people	5.9
Gaining greater involvement by members	5.9
Implementing change	5.8
Administration	5.2

Church politics	5.0
Developing a sense of community within the congregation	4.6
Relational difficulties among members of the congregation	4.5
Relational difficulties between leaders and the congregation	3.9
Relational difficulties between leaders	3.8
Counselling	3.8

Averages, however, can be misleading. An analysis of those who rated their problems or frustrations at the higher end of the scale (7–10) revealed the following percentages:

Issue	Average	Scale 7–10	Scale 8–10	Scale 9–10
How to do effective outreach	6.3	46%	34%	18%
Lack of commitment	5.9	41%	20%	7%
Low level of spiritual maturity	5.9	38%	20%	7%
Gaining greater involvement	5.9	40%	21%	8%
Implementing change	5.8	42%	26%	10%
Administration	5.2	28%	19%	12%
Church politics	5.0	33%	20%	14%
Developing a sense of community	4.6	21%	11%	3%
Difficulties among members	4.5	21%	12%	7%
Difficulties – leaders and congregation	3.9	17%	12%	7%
Difficulties between leaders	3.8	16%	12%	8%
Counselling	3.8	13%	7%	1%

Significantly, for one in five ministers church politics (i.e. power games) is one of the key problems – indeed, 14% of ministers rate it at either 9 or 10 on the scale of 0–10.

For ministers of larger churches problems related to power are even more acute (NB underlining shows where there is an increase in perception of difficulty):

Issue	Average	Scale 7–10	Scale 8–10	Scale 9–10
How to do effective outreach	6.3	35%	26%	6%
Implementing change	6.1	49%	27%	11%
Lack of commitment	5.9	36%	15%	4%
Low level of spiritual maturity	5.7	33%	17%	4%
Gaining greater involvement	5.7	35%	11%	2%
Church politics	5.5	40%	22%	13%
Developing a sense of community	5.2	22%	19%	2%
Administration	5.1	26%	17%	13%
Difficulties among members	4.8	29%	11%	4%
Difficulties – leaders and congregation	4.6	29%	22%	8%
Counselling	4.4	18%	9%	2%
Difficulties between leaders	4.1	20%	16%	7%

The task of implementing change poses more of a problem. For not only has the implementation moved up from fifth position to second position on the scale of averages, for almost half the ministers of larger churches (49%) the implementation of change is now ranked as high as 7–10 on the scale of difficulty. Almost as many (40%) rank church politics as between 7–10 on the scale of difficulty.

It is interesting to compare our results with the results produced by Barna's survey question about the major difficulties and frustrations of senior American pastors:[17]

Lack of laity commitment	30%
Handling financial and administrative duties	13%
How to do effective outreach	12%
Implementing change	10%
Counselling	9%
Developing community within the congregation	8%

---

[17] George Barna, *Today's Pastors* 66.

Low level of people's spiritual maturity	8%
Gaining greater leadership involvement by the laity	7%
Church politics	4%
Relational difficulties	4%

The British survey shows issues such as change and church politics as posing far more problems than they apparently do in America. That gives food for thought!

3. Leadership styles

3.1 Personality

The first question in this section asked ministers to name their personality type:

Personality
| High-key aggressive | 27% |
| Low-key, laid back | 69% |

The figures change quite markedly when we compare ministers of smaller with those of larger churches. In smaller churches (less than 150 at Sunday service) the percentage of ministers seeing themselves as 'high-key, aggressive' dropped to 20%, while those seeing themselves as 'low-key, laid-back' rose to 77%. By contrast in larger churches the percentage of ministers who saw themselves as 'high-key, aggressive' rose to 42%, with only 53% seeing themselves as 'low-key, laid-back'.

Possibly the linking of the term 'aggressive' to 'high-key' was unfortunate. The word 'aggressive' tends to have negative implications. But 'high-key' personality-types are not necessarily any worse than 'low-key' types. Indeed, God often uses dynamic and vibrant personalities to be very effective leaders. And yet, as with all personalities, there is this possible shadow-side.

3.2 Leadership style

Again there was a noticeable difference of response between ministers of smaller and larger churches.

	All ministers	Smaller	Larger
Autocratic	3%	4%	0%
Persuasive	32%	26%	44%
Consultative	44%	48%	36%
Participative	21%	21%	20%

In larger churches there is less consultation and more persuasion!

When church officials were asked to describe the leadership styles of their ministers (and here there was no distinction between smaller or larger churches), a slightly different picture emerged:

Autocratic	11%
Persuasive	36%
Consultative	36%
Participative	17%

Apparently church officials perceive a significantly higher proportion of ministers as autocratic and persuasive in style.

A similar difference in perception between ministers and church officials is to be found in the response to the question: 'Do you (does your minister) more often try to help people say what they think or say what you (your minister) thinks right away?'

	Ministers	Church officials
Help people say what they think	86%	70%
Say what they think right away	11%	22%

Although the majority of ministers appear to be good listeners, nonetheless church officials view one in five ministers as having a fairly directive approach.

Leaders or managers?

By and large ministers see themselves as leaders of people (67% – rising to 71% for ministers of larger churches) rather than managers of a process (28% – reducing to 24% for ministers of larger churches). And thank God they do! Because in a voluntary organization such as a church, leadership, which concentrates on people, is always more important than management, which focuses on the activity of a process. Bruce Reed puts it this way:

> In a 'socio-psychological' system, where people are the throughput in a 'socio-technical system' (the throughputs are material not human) leadership is of special importance, but because churches are voluntary where the through-put themselves provide many human and material resources, leadership is even of more importance.[18]

Vision

The vast majority of ministers (87%) claimed to have a clear sense of vision for the life of their church – and this was confirmed by the church officials (83%). Yet when asked to produce a brief statement of their vision, the vision statements seemed to be more like a general mission statement:

* 'To encourage each other as we share God's love and gifts in order to build up his church and proclaim the good news of Christ'
* 'To be the body of Christ in our community'

With two exceptions the nearest the many vision statements (only a selection of which have been quoted) came to being specific were the following three:

* 'To become a twenty-first-century-related post-modern missionary congregation'
* 'To develop a city-centre ministry'
* 'To respond to goals currently agreed by PCC'

---

[18] Bruce Reed, *The Dynamics of Religion* (Darton, Longman & Todd, London 1978) 165,166.

There were only two ministers who seemed to have developed a specific vision for their present ministry. One spoke of his desire to 'see the church move forward in appointing my successor, whilst keeping its focus on growth and service'. The second referred to a 'building scheme', which involved 'opening the doors of the church seven days a week'.

This general vagueness gives further cause for concern. If ministers do not have a clear sense of where they believe God wishes them to lead the church, then their churches are likely to make little progress. It is vision which gives direction, which in turn ensures that the energies of the church are rightly harnessed as the church seeks to fulfil its mission. The difference between vision and mission is that mission refers to the common calling of the church of God at large, whereas vision refers to the way in which that mission may be implemented in a particular church.

Mission and mission statements

Related to vision is the developing of a 'mission statement' for the church. Some 52% of both ministers and church officials agree that their church has a mission statement. On the one hand that is bad news: it means that just under half of the churches do not have an agreed goal at which they are seeking to aim. Yet on reflection it may in fact be very encouraging that over half the churches in question have in fact sought to encapsulate their vision for ministry into an agreed form of words. On the whole, however, it tends to be the larger churches (69%) rather than the smaller churches (44%) which have developed such a statement.

Some were unacceptably vague:

- 'To bring glory to God on earth as in heaven'
- 'To be an agent for the growth of the Kingdom of God'
- 'To serve Christ in the locality and in the world'

Some of the statements were delightfully snappy: e.g.

- 'To know Christ and make Christ known'
- 'To make the power and love of Jesus known'

- 'Strong enough to care, strong enough to share'
- 'To go Christ's way and make disciples'
- 'Telling the story and living the life'

Words, however, are not enough. Mission statements must be owned by the church if they are to be put into action. It is all very well having some snappy phrase on the church letter-head or notice-sheet, but until it penetrates the minds and hearts of the church as a whole, it is of little use.

It appears that in around half of those churches that have developed mission statements, the mission statement has been firmly rooted into the life of the church: 46% of ministers (50% of church officials) believe that for the most part their church fulfils that mission. If so, then a quarter of the churches in our survey must really be performing well!

Church agenda
To what extent, however, do church agendas reflect such mission statements? Perhaps not surprisingly, churches find it difficult to put ideals into action.

Church meetings illustrate this problem. It is good news that 11% of ministers (but 19% of church officials) said that three quarters of the agenda of their church meetings revolves around issues of mission, while only one quarter revolves around issues of maintenance such as finance and fabric.

On the other hand, 53% of ministers (46% of church officials) said that half the agenda revolves around issues of mission, with the other half focusing on issues of maintenance.

More depressingly, a further 31% of ministers (and of church officials) said that only one quarter of the agenda revolves around issues of mission, with three-quarters revolving around maintenance.

The 1% of churches where the agenda totally revolved around mission was balanced by the 1% where the agenda totally revolved around maintenance!

4. Ministerial accountability

To whom are ministers accountable?

Responses to questions relating to ministerial accountability were extremely varied. This was true even of the 57 Baptist ministers, all of whom one might suppose would be working within a similar framework. The responses of church officials were equally varied on this question.

If anything, there was a tendency on the part of the church officials to view the ministers as being slightly more godly than the ministers actually perceived themselves to be:

	Ministers	Church officials
Accountable to God	6%	7%
Accountable to self/no one	15%	4%
Accountable to church	30%	45%
Accountable to deacons/elders/ PCC/leaders	42%	45%

Unfortunately we did not ask respondents to define what they meant by accountability. Generally speaking, accountability appears to be a myth. Ministers by and large have few restrictions put upon them. Put crudely, provided they 'pay the rent' by conducting the services and by visiting some of the key members of the church, they can often get away with 'blue murder' if they wish. To be fair, few ministers would ever approach their ministry in this way. On the other hand, George Barna's observations of the American scene are equally true of the British scene:

> We essentially do not have an intelligent and reliable means of holding pastors accountable to perform as leaders of the flock. Beyond being in the pulpit a specified number of times, conducting himself properly with members of the congregation and managing staff and meetings

as they occur, few standards exist by which the pastor's performance is examined.[19]

This surely is not good, neither for the minister nor for the church. This lack of accountability is tantamount to an invitation to the abuse of power.

Job description

In any other context accountability would involve having a meaningful job description. However, 77% of ministers said they had no formal job description. Interestingly, 27% of church officials said they did not know if their minister had a job description! But how can one give account of one's ministry, where there are no agreed expectations? There seems to be a groundless assumption that everybody knows what a minister's job is about, whereas the actual truth is precisely the opposite. Indeed, even ministers themselves seem to be uncertain of what their role is.[20]

Appraisal

It was somewhat surprising to find that as many as 36% of ministers said they underwent regular appraisal. This is surprising, since one might well question how appraisal is possible where there is no job description.

Rather unexpected was the fact that a greater percentage of ministers in smaller churches underwent appraisal than ministers in larger churches. One might have thought that the ministers of larger churches would have been a little more business-like. As it is, as many as 71% of ministers of larger churches underwent no regular appraisal, as distinct from 60% of ministers of smaller churches.

But generally speaking most ministers, whether in smaller or larger churches, do not undergo regular appraisal. Here again is

---

[19] George Barna, *Today's Pastors* 146.
[20] See Paul Beasley-Murray, *Pastors Under Pressure* (Kingsway, Eastbourne 1989) 33,34.

a cause for concern. It is true that many ministers are not keen on the idea of being held to account. On the other hand, Jesus has a lot to say about the need for his followers to be good managers ('stewards'). There is a place for sitting down and asking searching questions about ministry.

Unfortunately ministers can be too jealous of their independence. Although the House of Lords may be correct in stating that a pastor's 'duties are defined and his activities are dictated not by contract but by conscience' (Davies v Presbyterian Church of Wales 1986), nonetheless there is something to be said for ministers having to give an account of their ministry to the church. Such a giving of an account need not be threatening, but liberating. One of the chief benefits of appraisal for me is that I feel that my fellow leaders can understand more clearly how I perceive my calling, and how I struggle to fulfil that calling.

Frequency of appraisal varied a good deal:

Frequency of appraisal	
Annually	13%
Six-monthly or less	5%
Every 18 months	2%
Every 2 or 3 years	7%
Every 3 to 5 years	67%

From personal experience I question the value of being appraised only now and again. As one committed to annual appraisal I have found it very helpful to think through my own personal ministry goals for the coming year – doing it with others has brought an extra degree of realism which otherwise I might not have had (the setting of too ambitious goals can prove disheartening). A further very positive benefit is that my fellow leaders use appraisal as an occasion to express their appreciation for my efforts. It's good to hear that appreciation not just every two or three years, but on an annual basis! Yet another benefit is that within the appraisal process there is a safe place to bring up some of one's frustrations about ministry. Again I have found it helpful to do so on an annual basis.[21]

Appraisals, however, are not necessarily conducted by one's fellow leaders. Indeed, in the survey only 6% have them done by church leaders such as deacons, elders, or church officers. Others, presumably Anglicans, were appraised by the bishop or archdeacon (8%). Yet other were appraised by their peers (2%) or by a ministerial support team (3%). Accompanied self- appraisal – favoured by Methodists – was the case for 4% of ministers.

Regular meetings with outside 'consultants'

With spiritual director	9%
With a supervisor	13%
With a therapist	4%
With a work consultant	7%

Many ministers have little external support. Those who do have such support tend to be ministers of larger churches

External support	Larger churches	Smaller churches
Spiritual director	29%	15%
Supervisor	22%	9%
Therapist	7%	3%

The exception here is that 8% of ministers of smaller churches meet with a work consultant as distinct from 4% of ministers of larger churches; however, we are dealing with such small figures, that statistically these figures have little significance.

The overall thrust of all these figures indicates that most ministers are on their own as far as their job is concerned. Meaningful external support, which involves some form of real accountability, is lacking.

Here is yet another major cause for concern. In almost any other caring profession supervision is the norm – indeed, in the

---

[21] See Paul Beasley-Murray, 'A British experience of appraisal', *Ministry Today* 8 (Feb 1997) 24-28.

counselling profession people are not recognized as qualified nor are they allowed to work with 'clients' unless they are in supervision. Yet ministers are able to counsel people haphazardly. Although supervision is no guarantee that abuse of one kind or another will not take place, it does provide regular opportunities for carers to reflect on their handling of their 'clients'. In turn this enables them to become more aware, both of themselves and also of the dynamics of the relationship involved. Where there is supervision, the risks of abuse are lessened.

Similarly, meeting with a spiritual director on a regular basis can be of great help, not least in dealing with this issue of the abuse of power. For where there is real honesty and openness on the part of the minister, and skill and perception on the part of the spiritual director, not only actions but also motives can be ruthlessly examined from a spiritual perspective. It is easy to deceive oneself – but in the presence of a godly man or woman such deceit can often be laid bare. But spiritual direction involves more than self-examination; it also offers a way of finding resources in God for the business of daily living. And how those resources are needed in ministry – not least when one is at the receiving end of abuse!

Therapy too can prove supportive. In some circles therapy is just a fad – not unlike colonic irrigation! Rightly understood, however, therapy offers one an opportunity to deal with the hurts and buffetings of life. Sadly, hurts and buffetings can often be a daily experience as far as ministry is concerned – although admittedly not all the time, thank God! And yet there are times in ministry when life becomes rough and ministers find themselves the losers in power struggles of one kind or another. Mugging is experienced not only on inner-city streets; it happens, at least on an emotional basis, in many a church. Seeking therapy at such a time is not merely following one of the fashions of the day; it is just common-sense. Of course therapy is more than simply massaging bruised emotions – it also presents an opportunity to explore one's feelings. In so doing, one may discover not simply healing, but also a degree of self-awareness, which in turn can throw light on issues of power and of accountability.

In a profession where most people work on their own, work consultants can be helpful in bringing perspective and advice to the tasks in hand. It is, for instance, easy for ministers to abuse their position through lack of balance. Work consultants can not only point to resources, but can also provide a form of 'quality-control' in ministry.

All these varieties of external 'consultancy' offer forms of support. And support is vital amidst the vortex of human emotions and ambitions to be found in many a church. But these systems of external 'consultancy' can also offer opportunities for self-examination and self-awareness. This too is a vital contribution if ministers are not to unduly impose themselves on their people. The fact is that our motivation for helping people is not always as selfless as it may appear. As Adolf Guggenbuehl-Craig rightly points out: 'No one can act out of exclusively pure motives. Even the noblest deeds are based on pure and impure, light and dark motivations.'[22] Similarly Peter Hawkins and Robin Shohet answer the question 'Why be a helper?' not only by acknowledging that 'for most of us the answer would include the wish to care, to cure, to heal', but by suggesting that 'alongside this, however, may be the hidden need for power, both in surrounding oneself with people worse off, and being able to direct parts of the lives of the people who need help'.[23] This is what psychologists call the 'power shadow'. It is vital that all who deal with people – and not least ministers – become aware of their vulnerability in this area. For ministers to turn to external consultants for help is a sign not of weakness, but of integrity.

Support groups

Some 26% of all ministers volunteered that they have access to some other kind of support network such as a fraternal or peer group. However, one might well question how meaningful such support is. Fraternals can be seed-beds of jealousy, and are

---

[22] Adolf Guggenbuehl-Craig, *Power in the Helping Professions* 10,11.
[23] Peter Hawkins & Robert Shohet, *Supervision in the Helping Professions* (Open University Press, Milton Keynes 1989) 11.

probably the last situation where most ministers would wish to make themselves vulnerable by being real and honest about themselves or the difficulties that they face. Support groups made up of friends who are committed to one another can be much more helpful; yet although such groups may offer safety and confidentiality, release and appreciation, they rarely provide much in terms of self-awareness or in terms of accountability.

5. Relationships in the church

Generally speaking the relationships of ministers with their churches seem to be very good.

Ministers' relationships with church staff

	Ministers	Church officials
Very good	40%	55%
Quite good	20%	21%
Satisfactory	5%	7%
Not very good	1%	4%
Not at all good	1%	0

Understandably a large number of respondents (33%) were not able to comment on the relationship of the minister with the church staff, for the simple reason that many churches are not in the financial position to be able to appoint anybody beyond the minister.

On what is thus an admittedly smaller statistical base, the relationships seemed to change slightly for the worse when relationships were rated with ministerial colleagues who formed part of the church staff:

Relationships with church staff in larger churches

	Ministers	Church officials
Very good	21%	21%
Quite good	14%	10%
Satisfactory	2%	6%

Not very good	3%		1%
Not at all good			2%

These figures confirm observations from other surveys that ministers are not the best of team players as far as their colleagues are concerned. Indeed, as we shall see from the later section on conflict, relationships do often break down between ministers working together in the same church. In part this may be because most ministers look forward to being a 'number one' – there are few long-term 'number twos' in ministry. Curacies, as also most 'assistantships', are training posts. The norm is for ministers to be in pastoral charge. True, occasionally one comes across genuine 'associate' pastors (as distinct from 'assistant' ministers who for reasons of status often prefer to be called 'associates') who have already had experience of being in pastoral charge and have now opted to become part of a ministerial team. But such 'associates' are very much the exception. Ministers generally find it difficult to play 'second fiddle'. They expect to be 'prima donnas'. For many, therefore, it is natural to exercise power.

Minister's' relationships with lay leaders

	Ministers	Church officials
Very good	50%	56%
Quite good	38%	29%
Satisfactory	5%	6%
Not very good	2%	4%

Relationships between ministers and their lay leaders appear to be a little better than relationships between ministers.

Ministers' relationships with the church in general

	Ministers	Church officials
Very good	38%	46%
Quite good	51%	38%
Satisfactory	9%	12%
Not very good	0	4%

As one might expect, the relationship between ministers and the church in general was not quite so warm as the relationship between ministers and leaders. Church officials were perhaps a little more generous in their estimation. This was true too when it came to rating other attributes of their ministers.

Minister's gentleness/compassion

	Ministers	Church officials
Very much	28%	0
To some extent	60%	88%

Minister's approachability

	Ministers	Church officials
Very much	40%	54%
To some extent	55%	34%

Minister's popularity

	Ministers	Church officials
Very much	22%	46%
To some extent	65%	38%

In spite of such popularity ministers feel they have few friends in the church

Friends

No close friends	40%*
No more than 5 close friends	26%
No more than 2 close friends	9%

*31% under forty-five; 51% over forty-five

Clearly many ministers are lonely people. The priest, wrote Henri Nouwen,

> [in]being friendly to everybody, very often has no friends himself. Always consulting and giving advice, he often has nobody to go to with his own pains and problems . . . [So] looking for acceptance, he tends to cling to his own counselees . . . He spends long hours with

them, more to fulfil his own desires than theirs. The paradox is that he who is taught to love everybody, in reality finds himself without any friends.[24]

Although Nouwen was referring primarily to Roman Catholic clergy, the ministerial loneliness is not restricted to any one denomination. Indeed, until very recently it was standard teaching at many a theological college that pastors should not have friends in the parish, lest they be perceived as having favourites.

In addition relationships between ministers and their people are in general less honest than they might be.

Openness

	Ministers	Church officials
Very able to speak the truth in love	27%	39%
Very able to receive criticism	15%	13%
Very able to express anger	5%	13%
Very able to publicly disagree with others	15%	38%
People very able to disagree with minister	18%	21%
Very much enjoy the clash of ideas	10%	12%.
Never sweep issues under the carpet	21%	32%
Very much tend to confront people on issues	5%	15%

The result is that only 13% of ministers (church officials: 28%) think that the church is very open and honest; furthermore

---

[24] Henri Nouwen, quoted by Rowland Croucher, *Renewal in the Pastorate* (an unpublished D.Min.Dissertation, Fuller Theological Seminary, Pasadena 1983) 23.

ministers believe that only 12% of their people believe that they are open and honest (church officials: 28%).

It is true that all these figures greatly improve when we include the responses modified by the phrase 'to some extent'. Nonetheless the picture emerges of a host of fairly superficial communities. Until conflict of one kind or another erupts, church people tend to be polite to one another, but not 'real'. It is likely that if church people learnt to be more real with one another, conflicts would tend to be less devastating. As things are, pressure builds up beneath the surface, with the result that feelings emerge only when they are at bursting point.

Ministers' popularity

	Ministers	Church officials
very popular	22%	46%
quite popular	62%	38%

On the whole ministers thought of themselves as being popular in the church – indeed 37% those who said they enjoy ministry a lot thought they were very popular! Church officials tended to be much more positive in the evaluation of their ministers. On the other hand, 3% of church officials said their minister was not very popular, and 1% said their minister was not at all popular. No ministers put themselves in these last two categories!

Objections to appointment?
Although 77% of ministers (84% of church officials) said that there had been no strong objections to their appointment, 13% of ministers (and 11% of church officials) acknowledged there had been.

6. Relationships with the Opposite Sex

Sexual abuse by Christian leaders is a major issue, both in North America and now increasingly in the United Kingdom. So we included some questions about relationships with the opposite sex.[25]

Just over half of the ministers (52%) said they had special guidelines in dealing with members of the opposite sex.[26]

Guidelines in dealing with members of the opposite sex

Would not see members of the opposite sex on their own	26%
Would always have somebody else around	13%
Would avoid any kind of physical contact	8%

But in practice it is clear that not all ministers have followed their guidelines when counselling members of the opposite sex on their own.

Ignoring guidelines

Often	11%
Sometimes	44%
Rarely	32%
Never	12%

Touching and hugging

Often	20%*
Sometimes	44%
Rarely	28%
Never	8%§

*38% of charismatics
§4% under forty-five; 14% over forty-five

---

[25] A more detailed consideration of sexual abuse and Christian counselling in Britain is to be found in an unpublished MSc dissertation by Patricia Fouque: *The Power Dimension of Counselling: The impact of Christian biblical counselling on survivors of sexual abuse* (The Roehampton Institute of Higher Education, Dept of Psychology, University of Surrey 1993). A major American work in this area is *The Abuse of Power: A Theological Problem* (Abingdon Press, Nashville 1991) by James Newton Poling.

[26] In 1991 the Methodists published *Some Elements of Pastoral Practice*, a brief discussion document by Brian E.Beck.

Temptation and sexual misbehaviour

Significantly just over half (54%) of ministers felt they were particularly vulnerable to sexual temptation (11% much more than anybody else; 43% a bit more than anybody else).

When asked if in ministry they had ever been tempted to do anything sexually inappropriate with anyone a number admitted that they had indeed been tempted.

Sexual temptation
Often   1%
Sometimes   19%
Rarely   34%
Never   44%

Sadly, a number had succumbed to such temptation.

Inappropriate behaviour
Sometimes   7%
Rarely   14%

This is surely a cause for concern, and all the more so if one bears in mind the probability that most ministers would have found it difficult to answer this question with real honesty. Sexual abuse in ministry is a problem. In addition, it must be remembered that the ministers responding are those still in ministry. There are many more ministers guilty of sexual abuse who have had to resign from ministry.[27]

Although the figures produced in this survey are less detailed than those from a North American survey of 300 pastors they do not differ significantly.[28]

---

[27] Unfortunately there are no detailed statistics of the extent of sexual abuse by ministers in the UK. The 1992 Safety Net survey of adult Christian survivors of sexual abuse found that 31% of those perpetraing the abuse were practising Christians, and 10% were leaders or clergy. So Patricia Fouque, 'Abuse In Ministry', *Ministry Today* 10 (June 1997) 6.
[28] *Leadership* IX (Winter 1988) 12.

North American experience

Ministers who since they had been in local church ministry had done something with someone (not their spouse) that they felt was sexually inappropriate	23%
Ministers who had participated in other forms of sexual contact with someone other than their spouse, e.g. passionate kissing, fondling, mutual masturbation	18%
Ministers who had had sexual intercourse with someone other than their spouse	12%

Only 4% said they were found out.

One major difference, however, is that 70% of the American pastors in the survey said they thought that pastors are particularly vulnerable. It could be that the Americans are in this respect more realistic than the British.

As for the Roman Catholic Church, in a recent book Richard Sipe estimated that at any one time 20% of priests are involved in a sexual relationship with a woman – marked by a certain stability – or involved in a more or less identifiable pattern of sexual relationships.[29] He went on to quote the reflection of the German theologian Romano Guardini: 'The church is the cross on which Christ is crucified daily.'[30]

Dealing with sexual temptation

First, there needs to be a recognition of the peculiar vulnerability present to both parties in the pastoral counselling situation. In a secular context friendship between the counsellor and the client is well nigh taboo. However, in a church context friendship is far from unethical – indeed, the client may well be a member well known to the minister. Pastoral counselling tends to lack the distance of secular counselling. All the more need therefore for boundaries to be set and maintained!

---

[29] A.W.Richard Sipe, *Sex, Priests and Power: Anatomy of a Crisis* (Cassell, London 1995) 72.

[30] Sipe, *Sex, Priests and Power* 181.

Secondly, it needs to be recognized that where abuse takes place within a pastoral relationship, the pastor is always the abuser and never the victim. 'The pastor, preacher, father or mother in God is always in a position of power in relation to the seeker for help'.[31] Hence the importance for ministers to establish guidelines which may offer them protection from, for instance, those who seek to love God through the minister who has made God real to them.

One important guideline could, for instance, include establishing a set number of times one would see a person of the opposite sex before referring them on. Referring people on is not failure; it often is a mark of pastoral wisdom. Other guidelines may include never seeing a person of the opposite sex without the knowledge of someone else – and ensuring that the person seeking help is also aware that the pastoral encounter is in this sense not entirely private. Needless to say, this area of counselling people of the opposite sex is one instance where supervision can be helpful. Supervision offers the possibility of confronting ministers not only with how they handle the present problem of the person seeking help, but also of how they handle the issue of their own sexuality. In addition, a supervisor is more able to see and confront the minister's individual 'blind spots'.

---

[31] Malcolm Goodspeed, 'Eros: Icon or Idol? A Minister's Sexuality in Practice', *Ministry Today* 6 (February 1996) 31.

Chapter Four

Power Games: Examining Perceptions and Experiences

Having examined the 'power grid' in participating churches, we now turn to 'power games' – perceptions and experiences of power in the church.

In order to determine people's attitudes toward power respondents were asked to say how far they agreed or disagreed with two groups of statements, the first relating in a general way to power in the church, the second relating power specifically to pastoral leadership.

1. Perceptions of power in the church

'God wants us to be powerful because there is a lot God wants us to do'

	Strongly agree	Slightly agree	Strongly disagree	Slightly disagree
Ministers	16%	26%	21%	18%
Officials	28%	29%	14%	6%

The majority of church officials appear to be happy to work with powerful leaders!

The statement is a quotation from Roy Oswald:

Does God want us to be powerful or not? I contend that God does want us to be powerful. All of us are called in unique ways to be effective. There is no particular virtue in being impotent or ineffective. In order to be effective we need to be powerful. There is no way around this. If power is the ability to get something done, then we all are going to need lots of power, because there is a lot God wants us to do.[1]

Oswald recognizes that such power needs to be used 'with fear and trembling'. But he maintains that for leaders not to use the power available to them is to be like the lazy servant in the parable, who buried his master's talent.

Roy Oswald's comments on power are typical of others from North American Christian leaders. Peter Wagner, the American church growth guru, emphasizing the fact that 'strong pastoral leaders' are the first vital sign of a healthy, growing church, continues: 'Pastor, you should be the spark plug! . . . Pastor, don't be afraid of your power.'[2] In his introduction to a seminary textbook, Calvin Miller declares: 'If God has called you to lead, do so! All leadership is strong. Weak leadership is no leadership . . . Lead with power or do not call yourself a leader.'[3] Miller then goes on throughout his book to speak of 'power leadership' and 'power leaders'. Unfortunately such statements, unqualified, can be misleading. They can easily encourage the abuse of power.

'Power is not a dirty word'

	Strongly agree	Slightly agree	Strongly disagree	Slightly disagree
Ministers	19%	35%	8%	16%
Officials	15%	38%	4%	13%

A bare majority of ministers believe that 'power is not a dirty word'.

---

[1] Roy Oswald, *Power Analysis Of A Congregation* 2.

[2] Peter Wagner, *Your Church Can Grow* (Regal, Glendale, California 1976) 55–68.

[3] Calvin Miller, *The Empowered Leader* (Broadman & Holman Publishers, Nashville 1995) x,xi.

Once again, Roy Oswald is the source of this quotation: 'Power is not a dirty word. Power is the ability to mobilize resources, to be effective towards specific ends. In and of itself power is neither good nor evil.'[4]

To be fair, the kind of power Oswald has in mind is the power to empower others: 'The more I empower others, the more powerful everyone in my system is, and the more powerful I become.'[5] The emphasis, however, needs to be on the empowerment of others. This naturally leads us on to the third statement.

'The exercise of power can only be justified in the interests of empowering others'

	Strongly agree	Slightly agree	Strongly disagree	Slightly disagree
Ministers	30%	35%	5%	20%
Officials	18%	35%	6%	9%

More ministers, and to a slightly lesser extent most church officials, were positive about the use of power to empower others.

This statement is a slight adaptation of some words of Robert Runcie, the former Archbishop of Canterbury: 'The exercise of power can only be justified in the interests of empowering Christian men and women to be what God wants them to be.'[6] Runcie in fact dislikes the use of the word 'power'. He much prefers the term 'authority', which for him is a form of legitimate power which always has the good of others in view:

> Authority can enable us to grow. . . . Authority far from being a necessary evil, is a good concerned to channel, harmonise and thus maximise human riches. . . . While a string quartet can operate by itself, the richer the variety of instrumentalists you assemble for music-making, the greater the need for a conductor to weld all those excellencies into an orchestra.[7]

---

[4] Roy Oswald, *Power Analysis Of A Congregation* 3.

[5] Roy Oswald, *Power Analysis* 4.

[6] Robert Runcie, *Authority In Crisis* 27.

[7] Robert Runcie, *Authority In Crisis* 17,18.

Runcie is not alone in preferring to speak of authority rather than of power. The philosopher John Skinner, for instance, likewise preferred to contrast 'legitimate power' with 'coercive power'. He regarded 'authority' as basically being a tool to nurture others, pointing out that the verb root of the noun 'auctoritas', from which we gain our word authority, is the Latin verb *augere*, which means 'to increase, to cause to grow, to fertilize, to make fertile, to strengthen, to increase or to enlarge'.[8]

'Power is like salt water: the more you drink the thirstier you become'

	Strongly agree	Slightly agree	Strongly disagree	Slightly disagree
Ministers	22%	38%	5%	20%
Officials	17%	14%	10%	13%

Almost two thirds of ministers agreed with this proposition, which is taken from an essay by Charles Colson.[9]

A former adviser to President Nixon, Colson was subsequently jailed for his involvement in the Watergate conspiracy, so writes out of his own personal experience. He found that 'although power may begin as a means to an end, it soon becomes the end itself'.[10] Elsewhere he writes:

> The lure of power can separate the most resolute of Christians from the true nature of Christian leadership, which is service to others. . . . Nothing distinguishes the kingdoms of man from the kingdom of God more than their diametrically opposed views of the exercise of power. One seeks to control people, the other to serve people; one promotes self, the other prostrates self; one seeks prestige and position, the other lifts up the lowly and despised.[11]

---

[8] John E.Skinner, 'Ideology, Authority And Faith' 33–35 in *Authority In the Anglican Communion* (Anglican Book Centre, Toronto 1987) ed.by S.W.Sykes.

[9] Charles Colson, 'The Power Illusion' 27 in *Power Religion* ed. M.S.Horton.

[10] Charles Colson 'The Power Illusion' 26.

[11] Charles Colson, *Kingdoms in Conflict* (Zondervan, Grand Rapids 1987) 272.

Power for God's Sake

> *'Power tends to corrupt, and absolute power corrupts*
> *absolutely, and this is especially true of religion'*

	Strongly agree	Slightly agree	Strongly disagree	Slightly disagree
Ministers	39%	32%	4%	11%
Officials	24%	32%	14%	11%

It appears that ministers may be more aware than church officials of the dangers of power in the church. It was Lord Acton who wrote that 'power tends to corrupt and absolute power corrupts absolutely'.[12] However, it is Richard Foster who particularly links the corrupting nature of power to religion.[13] He explains the peculiarly corrupt nature of religious power by pointing to the danger of people identifying their opinions with the will of God. As we have already seen above, nothing is more dangerous or devilish than when people bring God onto their side. The religious dimension of power has an intensity not found elsewhere. It adds a sense of self-righteousness which is not open to reason. It is precisely because Christians involve God in their power struggles, that these struggles are often more vicious than ever they might be in the wider world. For if God is on my side, then the Devil must be on your side. The struggle becomes a battle to the death between good and evil. But as Foster says: 'Jesus Christ alone is always right. The rest of us must recognize our own foibles and frailties and seek to learn from the correction of others.'[14]

> *'Resorting to piety is a power play peculiar to Christians'*

	Strongly agree	Slightly agree	Strongly disagree	Slightly disagree
Ministers	18%	32%	12%	13%
Officials	8%	16%	25%	13%

A far greater proportion of ministers than of church officials agreed with this proposition. Does their experience – perhaps even

---

12 Lord Acton in a letter to Bishop Mandell Creighton 3rd April 1887.
13 Richard Foster, *Money, Sex And Power* 178.
14 Richard Foster, *Money, Sex And Power* 179.

their knowledge of themselves – make ministers more aware of power disguised as piety?

The statement comes from *The Religion of Power* by Cheryl Forbes. She continues: 'It is manipulation at its worst – and best, since it nearly always succeeds.'[15] She is surely right. It is much more difficult to disagree with a personal opinion than to disagree with a word from God. The statement, for instance, 'God has led me to tell you that . . .' carries tremendous power. True, Paul told the Corinthian church that the gift of discernment should always be exercised along with the gift of prophecy (1 Cor. 12). However, many Christians seem to find it difficult to exercise their mental faculties.

Apparent piety can indeed be a smoke-screen for quite impious motives. Fraser Watts, the Starbridge Lecturer in Theology and the Natural Sciences at the University of Cambridge, makes a similar point, but in a slightly different way: 'There are perhaps few things more distasteful than power-struggles in the Church being waged under the camouflage of theological disagreements.'[16] Would that church people could be more honest – with themselves and with others!

'The exercise of power always implies coercion and violence'

	Strongly agree	Slightly agree	Strongly disagree	Slightly disagree
Ministers	5%	16%	44%	21%
Officials	4%	7%	47%	21%

The majority of respondents were not prepared to view power in a totally negative light.

This is another quotation from Cheryl Forbes.[17] To be fair, the sentence taken out of context is probably a little bit misleading for Forbes constantly contrasts the exercise of authority with the exercise of power.

---

[15] Cheryl Forbes, *The Religion Of Power* 20.

[16] Fraser Watts, 'Enabling Authority: A Psychological Approach', *Modern Churchman*, NS 33.2 (1991) 15.

[17] Cheryl Forbes, *The Religion of Power* 85.

Power means insistence on what we want for no other reason than
that we want it; it means making other people follow us despite their
own wishes. Power is assumed, insensitive, dehumanising, and ultimately destructive. Authority, on the other hand, is positive, and
usually involves a right which has been conferred within strictly
controlled bounds.[18]

Clearly if power is illegitimate in nature, then it is open to coercion
and violence. It all depends on what one means by 'power'.

'Power is a serious problem in the church today'

	Strongly agree	Slightly agree	Strongly disagree	Slightly disagree
Ministers	18%	39%	8%	11%
Officials	9%	21%	10%	21%

The majority of ministers agreed with this proposition – but not
so the church officials. Maybe the ministers were again being
more honest about themselves, while the church officials were
giving their ministers the benefit of the doubt.

In fact the original form of this statement was: 'Power is the
most serious problem in Christianity today.'[19] These words of Ted
Engstrom repeatedly find an echo in one form or another.

The religion of Babylon (i.e. the religion of violence) . . . is thriving
as never before in every sector of contemporary American life, even
in our synagogues and churches.[20]

All the errors and misfortunes of the church are closely bound up
with the curse of power.[21]

When God looks at our world, God weeps. God weeps because the
lust for power has entrapped and corrupted the human spirit . . . The
most insidious, divisive, and wounding power is the power used in
the service of God.[22]

---

[18] Cheryl Forbes, *The Religion Of Power* 84.
[19] Quoted by Cheryl Forbes, *The Religion of Power* 89.
[20] Walter Wink, *Engaging The Powers*, 13.
[21] Paul Tournier, *The Violence Inside* 152.
[22] Henri Nouwen, *The Path Of Power* (Darton, Longman & Todd,
London 1995), 8,13.

The fact that the misuse and abuse of power may not always be as blatant in Britain as in North America does not make it any less of a problem. Indeed, it is precisely the fact that it is not always recognized which makes it so dangerous.

2. Perceptions of power in leadership

Here is another series of statements to which ministers and church officials were asked to respond:

'Ministers exercise too much power'

	Strongly agree	Slightly agree	Strongly disagree	Slightly disagree
Ministers	7%	35%	5%	20%
Officials	4%	21%	14%	22%

A marked difference between ministers and church officials emerged. Is this because ministers were more self-aware? Or because many church officials feel happy to work with powerful ministers?

So much depends upon one's definition of power. Some ministers have abrogated their leadership powers. They find it much more comfortable to 'go with the flow'. And, of course, that is true. To take the initiative, to be an 'agent of change', is an uncomfortable experience. The moment leaders raise their heads above the parapet they become the target for snipers. Some ministers have undoubtedly opted out and fulfilled rather the role of 'chaplains' to the flock. Would that they exercised power!

On the other hand, others have gone for overkill. Although Protestant churches have since the Reformation decried the power of the Pope, there have been many little popes in not least the most Protestant of Protestant churches. Some of the 'newer' churches have introduced heavy 'shepherding' practices which appear to be based far more on the life of David than the life of Jesus.

Generalizations are therefore difficult. 'It all depends!' One thing is certain, ministers have not sufficiently empowered others.

They have insufficiently encouraged the ministry of all believers. The second statement highlights this issue:

'Ministers need to delegate more'

	Strongly agree	Agree slightly	Disagree slightly
Ministers	49%	39%	1%
Officials	30%	45%	3%

Not surprisingly there was general agreement that ministers need to delegate more. However, there was also some evidence to suggest that ministers do not always practise what they preach in this respect. Perceptions of how much the ministers actually delegated varied:

How much delegation?

	A lot	Quite a lot	A moderate amount
Ministers	8%	33%	49%
Officials	5%	33%	40%

'Ministers need to be people-orientated, not goal-orientated'

	Strongly agree	Slightly agree	Strongly disagree	Slightly disagree
Ministers	33%	27%	1%	16%
Officials	38%	32%	1%	7%
Ministers of larger churches	22%	27%	0%	22%

There is significant divergence of view between church officials and ministers – and in particular between church officials and ministers of larger churches.

'Pastoral leadership is non-coercive'

	Strongly agree	Slightly agree	Strongly disagree	Slightly disagree
Ministers	35%	33%	0	17%
Officials	32%	28%	2%	13%

Some words of John Stuart Mill, the nineteenth-century English philosopher, are very apposite: 'The only purpose for which power can be rightfully exercised over any civilised community, against his will, is to prevent harm to others. His own good, either physical or moral, is not a sufficient warrant.'[23]

True pastoral leadership is always servant leadership, i.e. leadership based on the pattern of Jesus, the Servant King. Such servant-leadership can never be from 'above', it must always be from below. Paul brings this out in 1 Corinthians 16:15-16: 'Now brothers and sisters, you know that members of the household of Stephanas were the first converts in Achaia, and they have devoted themselves to the service of the saints; I urge you to put yourselves at the service of such people.' Submission always goes hand in hand with service.

Pastoral leadership must always respect the conscience of another. It should never force another to do something over which they are basically unhappy. In this context Peter's words are very relevant: 'Do not lord it over those in your charge' (1 Pet. 5:3).

Pastoral leadership is not based on the power of force, but rather upon the power of love. In the oft-quoted words of Napoleon: 'Alexander, Caesar, Charlemagne, and myself founded great empires; but upon what did the creations of our genius depend? Upon force. Jesus alone founded his empire upon love, and to this very day millions would die for him.' The fact is that where people feel themselves loved, time and again they will follow. 'Whom you would change', said Martin Luther King, 'you must first love.'

'Personal growth is more important than church growth'

	Strongly agree	*Slightly agree*	*Strongly disagree*	*Slightly disagree*
Ministers	14%	30%	5%	20%
Officials	23%	22%	9%	10%

---

[23] *On Liberty* (1859) chapter 1.

A large minority – but a minority nonetheless – agreed that personal growth is more important than church growth. On the other hand a significant number disagreed.

In this case those who neither agreed nor disagreed are surely right. Personal growth and church growth go hand in hand, the two sides of the same coin. In the Great Commission Jesus commands us to 'make disciples' (Matt. 28:19f.). Such disciple-making includes both numerical ('baptizing') and qualitative ('teaching') growth. The task of any minister is to ensure that an 'all-round' ministry is exercised in this respect.

'Ministers have a God-given authority to lead'

	Strongly agree	Slightly agree	Strongly disagree	Slightly disagree
Ministers	41%	38%	2%	6%
Officials	44%	36%	3%	7%

This proposition prompted general agreement.

'Churches benefit from strong leadership'

	Strongly agree	Slightly agree	Strongly disagree	Slightly disagree
Ministers	42%	40%	0	5%
Officials	44%	36%	0	%

Churches without strong leadership tend to self-destruct. This is because in any given church there are always a variety of human emotions and ambitions moving not far beneath the surface. The task of the leader is to ensure that the church is driven by the wind of God's Spirit, and not deflected by the currents below. The good leader works as a senior partner with other leaders to achieve the mission of the church, build the church together as a team in order to enable it to fulfil that mission, and at the same time meet the needs of individuals within the church.[24] The respondents in this

---

[24] This is the basic thesis of *Dynamic Leadership* by Paul Beasley-Murray.

survey realized a basic fact, namely that a church doesn't just happen. The church can live up to its calling only as gifts of leadership are exercised.

'The key to church growth is leadership'

	Strongly agree	Slightly agree	Strongly disagree	Slightly disagree
Ministers	30%	40%	11%	1%
Officials	35%	34%	6%	4%

Here also ministers and church officials were in general agreement, although some ministers disagreed strongly. Nevertheless, as Peter Wagner has shown, the key to a healthy growing church is strong pastoral leadership. The first of the 'vital signs' he identifies is 'a pastor who is a possibility thinker and whose dynamic leadership has been used to catalyze the entire church into action for growth.'[25] The truth of what Wagner says from a North American viewpoint has been confirmed for the UK scene.[26] All growing churches have strong leadership.

'Ministers should not be afraid to use their power'

	Strongly agree	Slightly agree	Strongly disagree	Slightly disagree
Ministers	13%	40%	21%	15%
Officials	15%	37%	12%	4%

Ministers and officials agree in registering somewhat cautious approval to this proposition. A significant minority of ministers, however, are unhappy about it.

'Good pastoral leadership is directive'

	Strongly agree	Slightly agree	Strongly disagree	Slightly disagree
Ministers	18%	25%	9%	28%
Officials	27%	29%	4%	16%

[25] Wagner, *Your Church Can Grow* 55–68.
[26] Paul Beasley-Murray & Alan Wilkinson, *Turning The Tide* 31–37.

Here again caution is in evidence – certainly from the ministers. Church officials seem more inclined to give their ministers the benefit of the doubt.

3. Power exercised in the church

How is power exercised? Martha Stortz, an American theologian, has suggested that there are three different dimensions of ministerial power:

- power 'over' – or co-ercive power
- power 'within' – charismatic power
- power 'with' – co-active power

She sees these various dimensions of power as reflecting the Trinity, equating 'power over' with God the Father, 'power within' with God the Spirit, and 'power with' with God the Son:

> A God who creates, judges, and preserves is also a God who is with us in the incarnation. This person of God informs how one exercises 'power over'. A God who sustains, surprises, reveals is also a God who enables and requires the kind of discernment necessary to distinguishing how one exercises 'power within'. A God with us, 'Emmanuel', who befriends, comforts, and challenges, is also a God who shows us how to befriend one another. This person of God informs how one exercises 'power with'.[27]

On this analysis, no one leadership style is more of God than another. Furthermore, each leadership style is open to abuse. Everything depends on how leaders exercise their power 'over' others, how they discipline power 'within', and how they share power 'with' friends in ministry.

It was this analysis which in part lay behind the question: 'How do you mostly tend to exercise power? Is it "over" people as you give a strong lead? Is it "within" the church by the inspiration of

---

[27] Martha Ellen Stortz, *Pastor Power* (Abingdon, Nashville 1993) 42.

your personality? Or is it "with" people as you in turn empower them?'

How is power exercised?

	Ministers	Officials
'Over' people	4%	13%
'Within' the church	46%	44%
'With' people	47%	38%

Although there is a general recognition that ministers have a God-given authority to lead, the response suggests that many ministers are rightly circumspect in how they exercise that power. The majority felt that they either exercised power 'within' the church by the inspiration of their personality or 'with' people as they in turn empower them. However, church officials apparently believe their ministers are stronger leaders than they realize!

Among the various categories of ministers, the charismatics scored the highest with 8% of ministers who tend to exercise power 'over' people. There appeared to be a clear difference of degree between ministers of smaller and larger churches: 43% of ministers in smaller churches said they tended to lead 'within' the church by inspiration as against 51% of ministers of larger churches; while 52% of ministers of smaller churches tend to exercise power 'with' people in order to empower them as against 38% of ministers of larger churches.

3.1 The abuse of power

We then sought to test rather more precisely how ministers exercise their power; we asked eight fairly specific questions relating to the abuse of ministerial power.

'To what extent have you been involved in –

1. imposing your own style of worship?
2. using your sexuality to help you get your own way?
3. being manipulative in church meetings in order to get your own way?
4. not providing a lead when it is needed?

5. pushing through a course of action that was unpopular?
6. playing on the guilt of members of the congregation?
7. "hiding behind God" in order to get your own way?
8. intimidating weaker people into a course of action?'

| | Ministers (Officials) | | | |
	Very often	Fairly Often	Rarely	Never
Imposed worship style	8% (15%)	46% (42%)	37% (31%)	8% (10%)
Used sexuality	0 (1%)	1% (2%)	23% (17%)	74% (78%)
Manipulated meetings	0 (4%)	9% (11%)	56% (42%)	35% (42%)
Given no lead	1% (2%)	26% (13%)	61% (48%)	8% (34%)
Forced course of action	0 (0)	13% (9%)	72% (50%)	13% (37%)
Played on guilt	0 (1%)	2% (4%)	40% (24%)	57% (66%)
Hid behind God	0 (1%)	2% (8%)	30% (6%)	64% (80%)
Intimidated weak	0 (0)	1% (6%)	26% (15%)	72% (75%)

As one would expect, most ministers tend to give very direct leadership in the area of worship. More than a quarter of ministers admitted to often failing to provide a lead when it was needed, although in this context church officials tend to view their ministers in a more kindly light. A not insignificant number of ministers admitted to fairly often pushing through a course of action that was unpopular, although here too church officials tend to be more kindly disposed in evaluating the actions of their ministers. Or is it that their ministers are more realistic?

By contrast church officials felt that ministers more often manipulated church meetings than the ministers were willing to admit!

The percentage of ministers admitting having often abused their power in other ways decreased dramatically, although a far from insignificant number of ministers admitted that at times they had played on the guilt of their members (42%), had 'hidden behind God' in order to get their own way (32%), had intimidated weaker people (27%), and had used their sexuality to get their own way (24%).

These statistics become even more disturbing when one recognizes that they probably do not tell the whole truth. The true number of ministers involved in major abuse is likely to be considerably higher. The lower figures in the survey may be due in part to the fact that some ministers may be lacking in self-awareness, and in part because some may be unwilling to face up to their misuse of power.

3.2 Where does power lie in the church?

So far we have focused primarily on the power of the minister, and yet power does not reside in the minister alone. Indeed, according to the responses received, in most churches it is not the minister who has most power, but rather the group of leaders represented by 'the elders', 'the deacons', 'the PCC'. The responses indicated that generally power is exerted by the following people in this descending order of strength:

1. Elders/deacons/PCC
2. The minister
3. The Holy Spirit (!)
4. The congregation/church meeting
5. Older established families in the church
6. Former leaders

However we analysed the questionnaires – whether by responses from all the ministers, responses from ministers of smaller churches, responses from ministers of larger churches, responses of church officials – the order of strength was always the same. The only exception were the Baptists who put the Church Meeting on a par with the Holy Spirit!

This assessment of where power lies contrasts somewhat starkly with the American scene. Darius Salter reports:

When we asked the pastors who wielded the most power within their churches, 18% noted the board, 7% the congregation, but 67% saw themselves as having the most decision-making power in their churches. Whether they do or not isn't the issue. The greatest portion of these pastors think and act as if the power of destiny is in their hands.[28]

The relative unimportance attached to 'former leaders' may be a little surprising. In many churches 'former leaders' can at times be a fairly powerful lobby. Lyle Schaller refers to them as the AAEOL Club, i.e. the Angry Alienated Ex-Old Leaders:

> While their numbers rarely exceed one or two or three %, the members of this informal "club" (it usually meets without prior announcement in a member's home) often can be highly vocal in articulating their unhappiness with the growing sea of strange faces they see around them in church.[29]

It can be difficult for older members to give up the reins of power. Some of them have been so used to being at the centre of 'power' in church life, that they resent feeling marginalized. Lacking in grace, they sometimes still seek to control the life of the church, even although they no longer have any formal position. It can take a degree of strength on the part of the present leaders not to be bullied or intimidated by such AAEOLs.

3.3 Where does the minister's power lie?

Another fascinating ordering occurred in response to the question where the minister's focal point of authority in the church lay.

	Ministers	Officials
1. The minister's calling from God	76%	75%
2. The minister's position	68%	75%

---

[28] Darius Salter, *What Really Happens In Ministry* 27.
[29] Lyle Schaller, *The Pastor And The People* 165.

3. The minister's expertise	42%	51%
4. The minister's personal charisma	28%	32%

In other words, for ministers and church officials alike, the prime focus of authority are the minister's calling and position – two 'givens' which every minister shares. Personal qualities seemed to be of less significance. Interestingly, even charismatic ministers listed the minister's personal charisma in fourth place!

The importance of the minister's call cannot be over emphasized. Time and again it is this sense of call which sustains ministers through some of the most difficult times. It was, as we have seen, their sense of call which caused many ministers not to leave the ministry. From this perspective the sense of call is good and positive.

However, everything that is good can also be twisted and used to base ends. According to Larry Ingram, the 'call' which involves an experience in which an individual sees him or herself set aside as God's messenger or God's agent, with responsibility to God in the first place rather than to the church, results in the minister within the 'congregational tradition' feeling 'an internal pressure to control affairs, which effectively complements the external motivation of being held responsible for the success of the church by the congregation'.[30] Indeed, he later argues that this sense of call results in manipulation. 'The more the socialization process confirms the uniqueness of the pastor's calling, the greater is his willingness to manipulate the congregation. A corollary is that pastors with more experience (more confirming experiences) are more willing to engage in manipulative techniques.'[31] Although Ingram's research is based on a study of Southern Baptist pastors in the States, it doesn't take too much

---

[30] Larry C.Ingram, 'Notes on pastoral power in the congregational tradition', *Journal for the Scientific Study of Religion* XIX.1 (March 1980) 44.

[31] Larry C.Ingram, 'Leadership, Democracy and Religion: Role Ambiguity among Pastors In Southern Baptist Churches', *Journal for the Scientific Study of Religion* XX.2 (June 1981) 125.

insight to realise that there could be parallels in churches in Britain too.

The position of ministers clearly lends itself to the exercise of power. By virtue of their ordination to the Christian ministry in general and by virtue of the church's calling of them to their present office, ministers have been given authority not only to preach and teach, but to lead the people of God out in their mission in the world. Furthermore, in an almost unparalleled manner, ministers are given freedom to enter into people's homes in the course of pastoral care and to have access into their lives. All this power comes from position.

The calling and position of the minister are basic to the minister's authority in the church. That calling and that position can be strengthened both through the minister's professional expertise as also through his personal 'charisma'. It is these two elements which normally account for the greater influence of one minister over against another. The impact of a sermon, for instance, is all the greater if it has been well-researched and well-prepared. But even the most well-written of sermons may lack power if the minister lacks charisma. In the words of Phillipps Brooks, preaching can be defined as 'truth through personality'. Or as Martyn Lloyd Jones put it, it is 'logic on fire'. The minister's calling and position are of little worth without the expertise and the personal charisma.

It is therefore rather surprising that these two sources of authority did not score more – and not least that the minister's personal charisma was ranked as low as it was. For Darius Salter is surely right: 'success in ministry' as far as the so-called 'man-in-the-pew' is concerned, 'is largely predicated on personality'.[32] Similarly Paul Harrison, on the basis of his study of the American Free Churches, writes: 'It is the minister with the dramatic personality who often gains a higher prestige than that which is accorded the official priests of other religious movements.'[33] One

---

[32]   Darius Salter, *What Really Happens In Ministry* 65.
[33]   Paul M.Harrison, *Authority and Power in the Free Church Tradition. A Social Case Study Of The American Baptist Convention* (Princeton University Press, Princeton 1959) 217.

explanation for the lower rating of personal 'charisma' in our survey may be that some ministers may prefer to externalize the focus of their power on the ground that the power is more than justifiable since it is linked in with the demands of the 'job'.

3.4 How powerful are ministers?

Do ministers really appreciate the power they have – not least the power that is bestowed on them by reason of their call and their position? The answer appears to be that the larger the church the more likely they are to appreciate their power – although not as much as their church officials.

	Very powerful	Moderately powerful
Ministers	5%	62%
Officials	13%	70%
Ministers – small churches	4%	58%
Ministers – large churches	7%	71%

Ministers are actually often more powerful than either they or their members give credit for. The fact is that Sunday by Sunday ministers are exercising power as they preach. At the very least they are constantly influencing the way in which people think about life. Furthermore, when there are issues at stake, ministers have the opportunity to define those issues in their preaching and to give guidance on how those issues might be resolved. Similarly, in an indirect fashion they are exercising power as they lead the worship in the sense that they (as opposed to their members) are in the 'spotlight'. The very fact, for instance, that in most churches it is the ministers who preside at the Lord's Table, enhances their prestige. Again, in their ministry of visiting the sick and the bereaved, ministers are often – albeit unconsciously – gaining in power, in the sense that ministerial support during periods of vulnerability often evokes a strong sense of gratitude, if not obligation, toward the minister. Ministers exercise considerable power as a result of their day-to-day ministry. The fact that only

5% of ministers perceive themselves as 'very powerful' may simply underline their ambivalent attitude towards power.

3.5 False expectations

Perhaps as a result of the difference in perception regarding the power of the minister, there was also a marked difference in the way in which ministers and church officials responded to a question about the extent false expectations were put on the minister.

	To a large extent	To some extent	Not at all
Ministers	15%	73%	9%
Officials	8%	54%	30%

Interestingly 93% of ministers under forty-five felt particularly under pressure of expectation – 18% to a large extent, and 75% to some extent.

The nature of these false expectations was not spelt out. Ministers are put onto pedestals. Not only are they expected to be good with young people, they are expected to be good with old people too. They are expected to see to all the needs of the members, but at the same time to develop an effective evangelistic ministry too. In the words of John Harris, 'Churches do not hire a pastor, not at first. They hire a knotted tangle of Messianic, erotic, parental wishes and hopes dropped crazy-quilt fashion on the shoulders of one finite, limited individual.'[34]

False expectations relate not just to how ministers use their time. Strange as it may seem, they also relate to the fact that in our broken society individuals may see the minister as the parent they never had. Edwin Friedman, for example, writes: 'Much of the negative and superpositive "transference" that we receive from members of our congregational family is a direct result of the "baggage" they failed to leave at home.' The result is that ministers automatically attract all kinds of misdirected 'heat'.

---

[34] John C.Harris, *Stress, Power & Ministry* 73.

Friedman goes on to say that some people either deify or crucify religious leaders. There is often no middle ground.[35]

3.6 Ministerial authority

The same difference in perception between ministers and church officials with regard to ministerial power probably accounts too for the difference of response to a question relating to whether the churches give the minister more authority than is actually theirs.

	To a large extent	To some extent	Not at all
Ministers	14%	60%	21%
Officials	7%	45%	44%

In spite of the differences, the majority of both ordained and lay respondents felt that ministers have more authority than is actually theirs. Interestingly the two groups of ministers which felt that they were not given more authority than their due were the under-forty-fives (27% not at all) and those who enjoy ministry quite a lot (27%).

Unfortunately in the end the question proved too vague. We do not know what was meant by 'too much authority'. Is it, for instance, that some ministers are uncomfortable in exercising leadership in the church?

Freedom not to follow a minister
How much freedom do churches have not to follow the lead of their minister?

	A lot	Quite a lot	A moderate amount	Not very much	None at all
Ministers	21%	49%	25%	3%	0
Officials	15%	38%	33%	9%	0

---

[35] Edwin H.Friedman, *Generation to Generation: Family Process In Church & Synagogue* (Guilford Press, New York & London) 1985 quoted in *Leadership* XIV (Winter 1993) 81,82.

Church officials seem to think that their ministers have more power than they realize. On the basis of the church officials' answers one might well presume that ministers are more than likely to get their own way.

3.7 Ministerial grace

What would happen if a minister felt very strongly that a course of action was of God, but the church felt otherwise?

	Accept church's decision	Ignore church's decision
Ministers	70%	21%
Officials	58%	3%

Did some of the church officials respond this way because they have a high opinion of their ministers' godliness – their minister would follow God's leading, whatever? Or did they respond like this because they felt their ministers could be stubborn?

Three questions sought to probe the ability of ministers to give way gracefully, to handle anger and to handle disappointment. At first sight there appeared to be very little overall difference between the response of the ministers and of the church officials

Giving way gracefully

	Very able	To some extent
Ministers	21%	72%
Officials	33%	49%

Handling anger

	Very able	To some extent
Ministers	26%	64%
Officials	55%	30%

Handling disappointment

	Very able	To some extent
Ministers	11%	58%
Officials	25%	54%

It is noticeable that the church officials have a higher opinion of their ministers as 'very able' to give way, and to handle anger and disappointment. Is this because ministers are more realistic with themselves?

4. Power experienced in change

If the church in the West is to survive, it must change. William Easum, Director of the Texas-based organisation 21st Century Strategies, makes this point by likening traditional churches to dinosaurs.

> Congregations whose membership has plateaued or is declining have much in common with dinosaurs. Both have great heritages. Both require enormous amounts of food. . . . Both became endangered species. . . . Like the dinosaur they have a voracious appetite. Much of their time, energy, and money is spent foraging for food (for themselves), so that little time is left to feed the unchurched. . . . Either their pride or their nearsightedness keeps them from changing the ways they minister to people. . . . All around are unchurched, hurting people. . . . But many refuse to change their methods and structures to minister to people where they are in ways they can understand. Like the dinosaur, their necks are too stiff or their eyes too nearsighted. Clearly God doesn't care if these congregations survive; but God passionately cares if they meet the spiritual needs of those God sends their way.[36]

Within a specifically British context a similar point has been made by Kent Professor Robin Gill, who with reference to the Prayer Book version of Psalms 102:6 likens traditional churches to the pelicans in St James's Park in central London – peculiar creatures, stranded in an environment not their own. They are 'awkward, out of place, angular, with a big mouth but little brain, demanding but inactive'. He concludes that:

---

[36] *Dancing with Dinosaurs: Ministry in a Hostile and Hurting World* (Abingdon, Nashville 1993).

Churches in Britain need to make urgent choices about structure and direction. If they are to cease being pelicans, they need to be much clearer about how they might be effective in present-day Britain. They need to be more single-minded about growth . . . about how they might reach the nine out of ten people in Britain who seldom or never go to church.[37]

It is gratifying to note that change has been a major factor in almost every church surveyed. In response to our questions we received a mass of data detailing 484 separate key changes which had taken place over the past five years. 91% of ministers gave such details: 4% mentioned one key change; 9% two key changes; 25% three key changes; 28% four key changes; and 26% five key changes. It is possible that details of yet further key changes would have been given, had room been given on the questionnaire!

The nature of the changes varied enormously. Here are a few examples:

- Change in worship style   81%
- Major redevelopment of buildings   21%
- Change to appearance of buildings   18%
- Change in Sunday School work   18%
- Introduction of new pastoral groups   18%
- Introduction of Alpha courses   15%
- Change in time of Sunday services   14%

These responses are encouraging. For change is essential for life and growth. Only in death is there no change. The fact that there has been so much change in the churches represented in this survey augurs well for their future. True, change for change's sake effects little. But change with effective mission in view is always to be welcomed.

The responses underline once again the importance of leadership. For in all the changes the ministers clearly played a key role, and appear to have been responsible for most of them; similarly

---

[37] Robin Gill, *A Vision For Growth: Why Your Church Doesn't have to be a Pelican in the Wilderness* (SPCK, London 1996) 3,7.

'lay' leaders in general (e.g. elders and deacons) appear also to have played a significant role in initiating change. Leaders are almost by definition agents of change.

The fact is that we live in a fast-changing world; the church must constantly be adapting to the world if she is to survive, let alone to flourish. And yet, adapting is perhaps not the right word. It gives the impression of a church always trying to catch up with where society is. Ideally, leaders need to become pro-active in their thinking, anticipating the changes which impinge upon our lives. Pastors may not have a monopoly in terms of foresight and insight, but unlike most others they have time to reflect on current and future trends and in the light of that reflection can bring to the church proposals for change of one kind of another.

It was clear from the survey that people had not always found change easy. But do they ever? Change is always uncomfortable – particularly when we may not ourselves have initiated it. However, 47% of the changes had now been very much owned by the church and 43% to some extent. Only 9% of changes had not really been owned by the church, with a further 2% not at all owned! In view of the fact that we are dealing with major change over a relatively short period, these responses are quite encouraging.

5. Power experienced in conflict

Where there is so much change, differences of opinion are only to be expected. Conflict also: 94% of ministers and 91% of church officials felt that some degree of conflict was inevitable in church life. Interestingly 87% of ministers and 76% of church officials said that in their experience conflict could be productive in church life.

The ministers were asked to elaborate on the ways in which, in their experience, conflict could be productive, and almost all did, but in so doing, a number supplied provisos such as 'if handled positively and sensitively' – 'if contained in love' – 'if personalities are not involved'. The positive side of conflict was expressed in various ways:

Conflict 'brings things out into the open', revealing not simply hopes and fears, but sometimes 'past hurts'. It 'discloses hidden agendas', as it 'gets people to say what they mean face-to-face rather than behind backs'. In this way it 'reveals what people do feel passionate about'.

'It forces people to address and work through the issues', and in so doing 'makes people consider other angles, viewpoints and facts and breaks prejudice'. It 'challenges complacency'. As a result 'it can lead to better understanding'. As minds are sharpened, 'ideas and directions emerge or are refined when "tested" by contrary views'.

Conflict 'helps people to feel heard and to own decisions'.

Conflict can also enhance relationships if handled maturely: 'if people can be open and honest, it can build confidence in one another'.

These ministers are right. Low-level conflict, which focuses on issues rather than upon personalities, can be extremely productive. Disagreement can be very much a sign of life. As Lynn Buzzard says:

> This is especially true if a church has any character of mission. If a church is more than just a *koinonia* group – if it in fact is moving toward something, then there's going to be debate about what that something is and how we get there and who's going to lead us.[38]

A church with no conflict is a church where nothing is happening. Churches without conflict are probably churches where the ministers are not doing their job in seeking to lead out the people of God in adventurous mission. Lynn Buzzard quotes Saul Alinsky: 'Change means movement, and movement means friction, and friction means heat, and heat means conflict. You just can't get the rocket off the ground discreetly and quietly.'[39]

Alternatively, churches where there is no conflict are in danger of ceasing to be churches, and instead are running the risk of

---

[38] Lynn Buzzard, 'War and Peace in the Local Church', *Leadership* IV.3 (Summer 1983) 21.
[39] Lynn Buzzard, *Leadership* IV.3 (Summer 1983) 22.

cultism. When Paul urges the church at Philippi to be 'of the same mind' (Phil. 2:2), he is not advocating the 'group-think' of George Orwell's *Nineteen Eighty-Four*. The 'one mind' of which Paul was speaking was the mind of Christ, who laid aside all pretensions to power and to glory. Sadly the leaders who urge their followers to be 'of one mind' are often more concerned with their own 'mind' on the matter rather than with Christ's mind – unlike Christ, they are very much concerned with their own pretensions to power and glory.

Conflict can therefore be a sign of life and of health in the church. However, there is a world of a difference between low-level and high-level conflict. The former involves disagreement. The latter involves a fight, in which the contestants are not merely concerned to win – as part of winning they may also want to get rid of the opposition. No church benefits from this kind of conflict

In this respect Bill Hybels, the senior pastor of Willowcreek Community Church, Chicago, has some wise words to say: 'We expect disagreement, forceful disagreement. So instead of unity, we use the word community.... The mark of community – true biblical unity – is not the absence of conflict. It is the presence of a reconciling spirit.'[40] The role of leadership is to ensure that conflict does not get out of control – that it is managed productively.

As far as major conflict in a church is concerned, just over half (52%) of the ministers said that in the course of their ministerial career they had experienced major conflict in a church of which they were minister. The ministers also judged that 57% of their predecessors in their present church had experienced major conflict. 58% of church officials likewise said that they had experienced major conflict in a church. For some strange reason as many as 80% of church treasurers responding said that they had experienced major conflict. However, in so far as we are dealing with a fairly small sample base (25) this could be just a statistical anomaly.

---

[40] Bill Hybels, 'Standing in the Crossfire', *Leadership* XIV.1 (Winter 1993) 14.

5.1 Experiences of conflict

The experiences of conflict were many and varied. The ministers' experiences can be summarized as follows:

- Disputes with individuals or groups of individuals
- Conflict around particular issues (e.g. buildings)
- Breakdown in relationships with lay leaders
- Contention about changes in worship (always a contentious issue)
- Disagreements about the use of church discipline
- Conflict with ministerial colleagues
- Differences of understanding of ministry (including women in ministry)

The church officials' responses did not differ greatly from those of the ministers.

5.2 Conflict analysed

The respondents were asked to analyse their experience of conflict, in the sense that they were asked about what did the conflict revolve.

	Ministers	Officials
Minister's leadership style	3%	39%
Minister's values[41]	38%	29%
Minister's competence	13%	17%
Minister's productivity	11%	15%
Other reasons	22%	18%

The 'other' causes were many and various: e.g. friction between families, the self-appointed authority of a family group, greed, the church's unwillingness to change; an issue not directly to do with the minister.

---

[41] Values include such things as minister's understanding of mission, worship, and theology.

Again it is interesting to compare these figures with North American research. According to Speed Leas, a leading expert in these matters, in situations where the pastorate was involuntarily terminated:

- In 46% the pastor's interpersonal competence was involved
- In 28% there was significant value conflict
- In 12% the issue was productivity
- In 9% the pastor was physically or mentally ill (most of these were alcoholics)
- Only in 6% was bad preaching one of the major causes of termination

Leas's comments: 'Often the pastor's leadership becomes the central issue, no matter what people are really fighting over. The pastor will be blamed for taking one side, for not taking a side, or for the fact that others are having conflict.'[42]

Were these conflicts resolved? The answers are revealing.

	Ministers	Officials
Resolved through compromise	8%	7%
Resolved through acceptance of change	28%	22%
Unresolved	23%	34%

This last statistic is a serious one. If one in four, even one in three, conflicts are unresolved, then surely the mission of the church must be affected?

Members leaving the church

Bearing in mind that we are dealing with explicitly major conflict, it is surprising that relatively few members left. Only 38% of ministers (church officials: 42%) said that members had resigned. What is more, in less than 9% of churches (church officials: 6%) had resignations resulting directly from these conflicts totalled more than 6% of the church. Possibly this is why such a relatively

---

[42] Speed Leas, 'Inside Church Fights', *Leadership* X.1 (Winter 1989) 15.

high percentage of conflicts have remained unresolved. For the sake of the church's health it would surely be wiser for dissidents to find another spiritual home.

Ministers leaving the church

A not inconsiderable number of ministers, however, have left their churches in unhappy circumstances. Of the ministers responding to the questionnaire around one in six ministers (16%) admitted to having left a church unhappily.

Only 4% admitted to having been actually forced out. In this respect the situation is very different from the USA. There a similar survey revealed that some 22.8% of pastors had been forced out.[43] In that American survey 43% of forced-out pastors said a 'faction' pushed them out, and 71% of those indicated that the faction forcing them out numbered ten or less. It doesn't take many wolfhounds to savage a shepherd! Only 20% of pastors who were forced out said the real reason for their leaving was made known to the entire congregation.

When asked whether their predecessor had left in unhappy circumstances 43% of all ministers (church officials: 38%) said they had. For Baptist ministers, this figure rose to 53%What is more, 44% of church officials appear to have experienced a minister leaving in unhappy circumstances.

Of those who themselves had experienced major conflict, the most common occasion when conflict had erupted was soon after the 'honeymoon' period had come to an end (ministers 32%; church officials 17%). The next most common time was around Christmas (13% – but only 3% of church officials). The appointment of a new staff member could also prove a flash point (ministers 11%; church officials 12%).

Of those who had experienced major conflict just over half said that they had been sustained by their fellow-leaders (57%), and by friends inside (54%) and outside (59%) the church. Again one senses a degree of loneliness and isolation.

---

[43] *Leadership* (Winter 1996) 42.

Unjust treatment

Many ministers felt that there had been times when they had been unjustly treated, but church officials were not so aware of such treatment. Interestingly, Baptist ministers in particular felt that they had been poorly treated.

	Ministers	Baptist ministers	Officials
Unjust treatment by individual members	73%	81%	59%
Unjust treatment by deacons/elders	28%	39%	20%
Unjust treatment by church staff	15%	16%	11%

The areas in which ministers had been treated unjustly were varied.

	Ministers	Officials
Unfair criticism behind one's back	57%	47%
Overload of expectation	45%	29%
Verbal attacks in a church meeting	36%	21%
Verbal attacks after a service	35%	26%
Unfair criticism to one's face	34%	26%.
Work overload	23%	12%
Sidelined/ganged up on	16%	12%
Forced by influential families	11%	11%
Threats of dismissal	5%	4%
Sexual manipulation	2%	0
Other	8%	5%

The expression of anger and the ability to forgive

In so far as many ministers appear to find it difficult to express their anger, it is perhaps not unexpected that less than a quarter (24%) felt able to express their anger to fellow leaders such as deacons and/or elders. Indeed, only 33% said they were able to make their anger known to their wives.

Perhaps precisely because ministers find it difficult to express anger, it is also not unexpected that a good number of ministers find it difficult to let go and forgive

	Ministers	Officials
To a large extent	56%	31%
To some extent	28%	27%

According to 31% of church officials, their ministers have just not been able to forgive. The fact is that there is no true forgiveness where anger is suppressed. Forgiveness by definition is a letting go. When ministers are unable to express their hurt and anger, the consequence normally is that they cannot truly forgive the one who has sinned against them.

6. Suffering

Ministers have experienced a wide variety of distress as a result of being in ministry. The following table also records church officials' awareness of ministers who haved suffered as a result of being in ministry.

	Ministers	Officials
Stress	92%	80%
Hurt	83%	64%
Hurt experienced by spouse	76%	45%
Sleeping difficulties	57%	31%
Abuse of spouse/family	55%	21%
Poor health	44%	56%
Suicidal thoughts	10%	2%
Depression	9%	10%
Nightmares	7%	4%

Not surprisingly, the church officials were mostly less aware than the ministers themselves, yet even so they knew of a good number of ministers who had suffered because of their ministry.

In the light of this catalogue of misery it may be surprising to discover that only 41% of ministers and 36% of church officials agreed that 'the church makes a lousy mother'. Any other institution with such a track record would hardly be commended for its caring qualities. Yet strangely, for all the church's failings, God's people do care. For although within the church there are some who abuse their leaders, there are others who deeply care for those who have been called to have pastoral charge of them.

But should one expect the church to care for its pastors? John Harris argues that pastors should seek to become autonomous to the point at which they no longer expect their churches to assume responsibility for their lives and well being.[44] It is precisely the dependency of pastors on their churches which causes them to be so vulnerable. Harris has a point. On the other hand, does not Paul's teaching on the Church as the Body of Christ (see 1 Cor. 12) run directly counter to this emphasis on autonomy? Autonomy may be safer and less vulnerable, but is not 'one-anotherness' of the essence of Christian community, a one-anotherness in which we are mutually dependent upon one another as we seek to go the way of Christ?

6.1 Venting one's temper

On occasion ministers may feel so seriously provoked that they vent their temper:

	Often	Sometimes	Rarely	Never
Preached aggressively	4%	45%	44%	7%
Lost temper with church in service	0	1%	15%	82%
Lost temper with church in church meeting	0	2%	38%	60%
Lost temper with individual in service	0	2%	12%	84%

---

[44] John C. Harris, *Stress, Power and Ministry* 128,129.

Lost temper with individual in church meeting	0	5%	38%	55%
Lost temper in one-to-one encounter	0	16%	45%	38%
Over-zealous in handling church discipline	0	3%	30%	65%

Church officials on the whole were a little kinder in their evaluation of their ministers. Their responses tended to underplay the wrath of the minister!

Whether all this restraint is always a good thing may be open to question. Sometimes emotion needs to be expressed if feelings are to be conveyed. Furthermore, the process of healing is frequently helped rather than hindered by the occasional expression of feelings. On the other hand, such feelings need to be discharged appropriately, both in terms of 'how' and 'with whom'. Otherwise innocent people get hurt, especially as the strength and intensity of emotion may well derive more from some other aspect of the minister's personal agenda than from its ostensible and immediate cause.

7. Power in the church – the survey in retrospect

From the numerous insights and the mass of data elicited by the survey, one thing in particular has emerged with crystal clarity: power is a serious problem in the church today. At first sight the survey may appear a fairly dry academic exercise; but some of its findings are deeply disturbing and challenging. Indeed, it supports headlines in the national press, not excluding the tabloids:

- 'Churches treat us badly' say nine out of ten ministers
- Most ministers under forty-five have considered giving up their calling
- One in six ministers leave their churches in 'unhappy circumstances'

- One in seven ministers confess to sexual misbehaviour
- One in five churches racked by power politics
- The myth of accountability in the church

As everybody knows, headlines can mislead. Inevitably they simplify. Yet it seems clear that the pressures of ministry are increasing, with the result that an unacceptable proportion of ministers are considering leaving the ministry. Although there is a good deal of satisfaction in ministry, nonetheless there is a good deal of unhappiness too.

But the unhappiness is not confined to ministers. Many members too must be unhappy. For, as we have seen, ministers are not simply victims of abuse: at times they themselves can be the abusers. Ministers can be manipulative, they can create false guilt, they can intimidate, they can 'hide behind God' to get their own way . . . In these ways – and many others – they can and do abuse their position, and in so doing abuse others. The upshot is that people feel blamed, responsible, sinful, bewildered, angry and very hurt. Some may leave the church, but many stay.

Where does the root of the problem lie? Why is it that in communities dedicated to the service of the Servant-King power games of one kind or another are such an issue? No doubt the ultimate root is to be found in the sinfulness of the human heart. Egocentricity is alive and well in the church almost as much as in the world. However, a contributing factor is that many – probably most – people have not thought through the issue of how power is handled in the church. The survey shows how both ministers and church officials display a good deal of uncertainty in their attitudes toward power. Most believe that power is not a dirty word, and yet at the same time they clearly recognize it to be a dangerous force. Most ministers believe that they have a God-given authority to lead, and yet they appear to be unsure as to the nature of that authority. Ministers appear to feel happiest when their use of power is linked to the empowerment of others, and yet the survey reveals that in reality they have a tendency to hold on to power.

It seems clear that church leaders are not a little confused in their thinking. So it is not surprising if their leadership is

sometimes questionable. In the following chapters we shall look
at some models for handling power in the church, and in
particular focus on the model presented by Jesus himself. We
shall then consider some even more practical ways in which
power can be handled in the church.

Chapter Five

Power Dimensions: Sizing-up Models

1. Analyses of power

There are many ways of analysing and defining power. This chapter examines a few examples, which in their varying ways bring out the multifaceted nature of power.

The American Centre For Leadership Studies[1] defines leadership as 'the process of attempting to influence the behaviour of others' and power 'the means by which the leader actionally gains the compliance of the follower(s)'. Since leaders cannot automatically influence other people, they must utilize power to succeed in their attempt to exercise influence. Such power may be derived from seven bases:

- Expert power: the perception that the leader has relevant education, experience, and expertise.
- Information power: the perceived access to – or possession of – useful information.
- Referent power: the perceived attractiveness of interacting with the leader.
- Legitimate power: the perception that it is appropriate for the leader to make decisions due to title, role, or position in the organization.

---

[1] *Power Perception Profile*, 1993, published in Europe by Management Learning Resources Ltd, PO Box 28, Carmarthen, SA31 1DT, UK.

- Reward power: the perceived ability to provide things that people would like to have.
- Connection power: the perceived association of the leader with influential persons or organizations.
- Coercive power: the perceived ability to provide sanctions, punishment or consequences for not performing.

A different approach is found in the work of Rollo May. He defined power as 'the ability to cause or prevent change' and distinguished five kinds of power:[2]

- Exploitative power: the most destructive kind of power, which always presupposes violence or the threat of violence.
- Manipulative power: i.e. power over another person
- Competitive power: i.e. power against another. In its negative form it consists of one person going up because his opponent goes down.
- Nutrient power: i.e. power for the other: e.g. teaching
- Integrative power: i.e. power with the other person. My power abets my neighbour's power

Roy Oswald adopted yet another approach, which is particularly helpful when we are seeking to analyse the power of lay leaders within a congregation. He first of all distinguishes power from authority: 'Authority is granted to people by the system through roles to be occupied. Power relates to individuals' ability to accomplish things outside or over above the authority given to them in roles'.[3] In terms of corporate power within the church, he argues that there are four currencies of power that are valued highly by most congregations:

- Reputational power is that power an organization gives to me because of its past experiences with me.

---

[2] Rollo May, *Power and Innocence: A Search for the Sources of Violence* (British Edition, Fontana/Collins, Glasgow 1976) 99–110.
[3] Roy Oswald, *Power Analysis of a Congregation* (Alban, Bethesda, Maryland 1981) 7.

- Coalitional power is mine when I am perceived as being part of a caucus or support group within the larger system.
- Communicational power is mine when I have access to important information within a system.
- Structural power is mine when I occupy a role that is part of the official structure of the parish.

More recently Martyn Percy, building on the theoretical work of the sociologist Stewart Clegg, has sought to analyse the character and framework of religious power in terms of circuits.[4] He writes:

> There are certain 'nodal points' or fundaments of belief and practice which conduct and direct the forces or forms of power. . . . These nodal points need orchestrating at times by controllers of power brokers (leaders).[5]

On this view power is far more than charisma, important though charisma may be.

> Power is inextricably linked to structure and is represented in the circuits of framework in a number of ways. Power is evidently present as each specified modality of episodic, dispositional and facilitative power. It is also present in the overall flow of action through the circuits of power, the relational articulation which will constitute the calibration of this flow.[6]

A very different approach is offered by the theologian Walter Wink.[7] Wink draws upon what the Bible calls the 'principalities and powers' to explain the spirituality of the life of an institution. These 'principalities and powers', sometimes described by the Apostle Paul as the 'elemental spirits of the world' (Gal. 4:3; Col.

---

[4] Stewart R. Clegg, *Frameworks of Power* (Sage Publications, London 1989), especially 187–240.

[5] Martyn Percy, *Words, Wonders and Power* 46.

[6] Martyn Percy, *Words, Wonders and Power* 50.

[7] Walter Wink, *Engaging the Powers* (Fortress Press, Minneapolis 1992).

2:8,20), are currently fallen powers. Wink uses this model to explain the fallenness of political, economic and cultural institutions. However, this model can equally be applied to churches. Indeed, it is this model which lies behind much of the present fundamentalist thinking about territorial spirits and spiritual warfare.[8] Whatever the terminology used, it cannot be denied that there are within many churches what one might also term 'institutional viruses' which seem constantly to undermine the spiritual health of those churches.

This emphasis on the fallenness of institutions is a salutary corrective to the bright-eyed and naïve idealism to be found in some of today's 'new' churches. However, it is also a reminder to every leader, as indeed to every church, of how easy it is for church life to be manipulated by forces which are hostile to Christ's way.

2. Models of power

Analyses of power deal with the theory, but models of power depict power in action. Such practical models are often easier to relate to than many a theoretical analysis.

Celia Hahn, for instance, of the North American Alban Institute, presents four models for exercising ministerial power by looking at four clergy, each of whom has found a distinct way to shape the role of ordained leadership:[9]

Jim Adams, rector of a large Washington Episcopalian church, localizes his authority in his *authenticity*. His authority comes from being 'real', from 'saying what I really think and feel'. 'As soon as I have a position, I try to state it calmly as just my opinion. Then I try to detach myself emotionally from my

---

[8] See, for instance, Peter Wagner, *Warfare Prayer* (Regal, Ventura, California 1992).

[9] Celia Allison Hahn, 'The Paradoxical Authority of Clergy: Four Stories', *Congregations* July–August 1994 14–18.

position so that other people can sharpen what they think'. In this way he seeks to give others the freedom and respect that he wants for himself.

Dee Crabtree, Senior Minister of a United Church of Christ in Colchester, sees her role as a *coach*, helping her people 'discover the authority of their own lives and possible ministries that they might have'. Passionate for the ministry of all God's people, not least beyond the walls of the church, she is convinced that 'the only way we can equip the saints is to honour them as saints'.

Dwight Lundgren, Senior Minister of a Baptist Church in Providence, Rhode Island, sees his role symbolized by his *robe* (gown). It stands for his theological training and professional expertise. But paradoxically it also signals that 'we're all fools for Christ'. He sees himself as 'a kind of a court jester', who handles Scripture in such a way as to make his listeners wonder about God and his place in their lives. In no way does he seek to dictate another person's pilgrimage.

For Dorothy McMahon, Minister of a Uniting Church in Sydney, Australia, her central understanding of ministry is that of a *priest*. Her ministry 'includes being humanly present to the people, staying open to God's grace, and bringing the sacraments to the people . . . she is a vehicle for the power which comes from beyond her. . . . She finds her power in pointing to the space where God and people meet'

The strength of Hahn's approach, summarized above, seems to be in the way in which the models are personalized. For most of us that is the way in which we tend to live. We model ourselves on others. For some ministers the model they seek to emulate may be a pastor who had a great influence on their lives in their teenage years; for others it may be some 'super pastor' of some 'mega church' whose ministry has attracted nation-wide if not world-wide attention. Models vary. The question is: do we have the right models? In all four of the models Celia Hahn presents there is truth applicable to every minister. And yet neither individually or corporately do the models fully satisfy.

3. Four models for ministry

A very different approach is found in the four models for ministry depicted by two thoughtful Southern Baptists, Joe Trull and James Carter.[10]

In the first place, there is the model of the *chief executive officer*. Some ministers aspire to be a spiritual CEO. The primary descriptive word here is 'active'. 'This leader makes things happen, no matter what it takes. Rather than actively doing ministry, this minister will often direct ministry.'

Secondly, and related to the first, is the model of the *political dictator*. The primary descriptive word is 'authoritative'. These ministers are authority figures who 'make their desires known to the congregation, often couching these desires in terms of the will of God or the direction that God has revealed to them, and expects them to carry out.' In this respect the amusing story is told of a pastor who together with his deacons was accused of running the church: 'There's not a word of truth in it,' he snorted, 'the deacons have nothing to do with it!'

Thirdly, there is the model of the *hired hand*. The primary descriptive word is 'passive'. Hired-hand type ministers exert little leadership. Instead they are subservient to the church board or to the church as a whole.

Fourthly, there is the preferred model – the model of *Jesus the servant*. The primary descriptive word is 'responsive'. 'The minister who acts as a servant responds to the needs of the people, responds to the directives of God, and responds to the guidance of the Holy Spirit.'

At first sight these four models may seem too trite. Expressed in these terms few ministers would do other than to opt for the 'preferred' model of Jesus the servant. And yet if ministers are honest, in practice many of them diverge from this Jesus model.

Ministers in larger churches are especially vulnerable to the temptation to adopt the trappings of a CEO. Indeed, at a private

---

[10] Joe E.Trull and James E.Carter, *Ministerial Ethics* (Broadman & Holman, Nashville 1993) 95–98.

consultation for ministers of churches with an active membership of 350 or more most of the ministers agreed that they felt uncomfortable with the term 'pastor'. They saw themselves as 'leaders' whose chief task was to make their churches grow. As leaders they were concerned above all with vision and strategy, not with pastoral care. Certainly pastoral visiting and knowing of all their members by name did not feature on their agenda. But is there not an imbalance here? Surely even leaders of large churches must have a pastoral heart for their people. Ministry patterned on the life of Jesus is always about serving people – the institution is secondary.

There is a breed of minister – found in both small and large churches – which brooks no questioning of their leadership. These charismatic figures, apparently incapable of self-questioning take over all the decision-making processes of the church. It is surprising how easily a church can be manipulated when the minister dresses up his (and it is almost always 'his') thoughts as a 'word from the Lord'. Those who disagree with their decisions are simply drummed out of the church – for they are deemed not just to have disagreed with the pastor, but to all intents and purposes to have disagreed with the Lord himself. In one case, after a couple had dared to question their pastor's leadership with another couple in one particular church, they were visited at night by two elders and told there and then to leave that church. This is surely a form of power-abuse. However strongly leaders may feel that they have discerned the mind of Christ on a particular matter, they must always give people freedom to disagree. Ministers who employ coercive tactics are deceiving themselves if they imagine that they are serving Christ.

Some of the saddest figures in ministry are the 'hired hands'. Often as a result of a past experience where their leadership was rejected, their ministry has deteriorated into meeting the needs and expectations of the church – or possibly of certain power-brokers in the church. Their ministry is limited to preaching and to pastoral care – they no longer seek to give direction to the church in its mission. They have abdicated their authority and the power inherent in that authority, and have become private chaplains to the flock. In fact, they have become the abused, rather than the abusers. And at the end of the day the cause of Christ is not furthered in this way. Ministry is more than serving people – it is in the first place serving God, whose concerns reach way beyond any local church.

4. The model of Paul

At many an ordination service the model of ministry which is set before the ordinands is one to be found within the writings of the Apostle Paul. The Pastoral Epistles, as the letters to Timothy and Titus have come to be known, are a happy hunting ground for those preaching sermons with ministers in view. So also, for that matter, is 2 Corinthians. It is true that Paul's ministry was 'translocal' and therefore wider than of most ministers, but there is no doubt that he saw himself as a pastor. His letters are a clear testimony to his pastoral heart. Indeed, the letters are themselves a product of his pastoral care, for through them Paul exercised a pastoral role toward the churches which he had founded.[11]

As his letters reveal, Paul was a forceful person, who often expected obedience from the churches in his care (e.g. 2 Cor. 10:6; Phil. 2:12; Philem. 2). His letters are full of instructions on how his readers were to live their lives together (e.g. 1 Cor. 11:17,34; 1 Thess. 4:2; 2 Thess. 3:6–15). However, he told the Corinthians that the 'authority' which the Lord had given him was for 'building up' the church, and not for 'tearing down' (2 Cor. 10:8; 13:10: cf. 12:19) – for it was only arguments (2 Cor. 10:3–5), and not people, which he sought to destroy.

It has often been assumed that Paul based his authority on his calling to be an apostle. However, at no point do we find him issuing instructions on the basis of his apostleship. It is much more

---

[11] See Ernest Best, *Paul and his Converts*, T & T Clark, Edinburgh 1988. Also Paul Beasley-Murray, 'Paul as Pastor' 654–658 in *Dictionary of Paul and his Letters* (IVP, Leicester & Downers Grove Illinois 1993) edited by G.F. Hawthorne & R.P. Martin.

likely that his sense of authority was derived from his position as the founding-father of his churches.[12]

But Paul put limits upon his own authority. He much preferred to 'appeal' (e.g. Rom. 12:1; 15:30; 16:17; 1 Cor. 1:10; 4:16; 16:16; 2 Cor. 5:20; 6:1; 10:1; 13:11; Eph. 4:1; Phil. 4:2; 1 Thess. 2:11; 4:1,10; 5:14; 2 Thess. 3:12) rather than to 'command', which in turn implies that he preferred not to impose his own will upon the churches, but rather to encourage them to make their own decisions. Hence he wrote to the Corinthians that he did not seek to 'lord it over your faith' (2 Cor. 1:24); and reminded the Galatians, 'You were called to freedom' (Gal. 5:13). The churches he founded may have been his spiritual children, but they were no longer babes in Christ. In this respect Paul's model was the parent/adult child, and not the parent/infant child. So although he was clear about the form of discipline which should be exercised at Corinth towards the man committing incest, he preferred that it be the church itself which exercised that discipline (1 Cor. 5). Paul did not want his children to be overly dependent upon him. In this particular respect he offers a very relevant model to leaders today.

In a recent monograph Anthony Bash has illustrated how Paul's ambassadorial language in 2 Corinthians 5:20 has nothing to do with power and strength, but rather presupposes weakness, need and dependence. It was in his role as Christ's ambassador that Paul 'appealed' to the Corinthians as indeed to others. Bash goes on to show that 'appeal was the primary way by which Paul chose to generate action and so exercise power'. The threats in 2 Corinthians 13:1–3 were out of character. 'The

---

[12] In this respect it should be born in mind that for Jews and Greeks alike the father relationship was perceived as one of authority. For a Jew, to honour one's father inevitably involved obedience (see 2 Kings 16:7: 'your servant and your son'). Epictetus declared: 'To be a son is to regard all one's possessions as the property of the father, to obey the father in all things, never to blame him before anyone, to support him with all one's power' (Epictetus, Diss II 107). In Roman society a father retained control over his children even after they were married.

overall impression in 2 Corinthians is of a man inwardly reflective and aware, conscious that he was accountable to God, not driven by self-aggrandizement; rather he was self-giving, broken and immensely loving'.[13]

In a later article Anthony Bash and Martyn Percy reflect further on Paul's use of this model of ambassador which is seen as a model for Christian ministry today.[14]

> What then is true Christian weakness? It is the powerlessness which arises from choosing to appeal for consent rather than to demand – and to compel – submission. It is the powerlessness which arises from choosing to exercise power other than by force. It is the powerlessness which arises from preferring to be rejected and to suffer than to impose and get one's way. It is also the powerlessness which Paul modelled.

Paul's model of ministry was in fact a reflection of self-emptying (*kenosis*) of Christ depicted in the Christ-hymn of Philippians 2:6–11. In the light of this self-emptying – both Paul's and Christ's – Anthony Bash and Martyn Percy helpfully draw the following conclusions for Christian ministry today:

> First, paraenetic appeal on the part of Christian ministers is an *imitatio* of the gospel and of the ministry of Christ. For if God himself in his incarnational form expressed himself to human beings in voluntary self-limitation and appealed to but did not compel, men and women to follow him, then Christian ministers must do the same. . . .
>
> Second, any appeal must be expressed in the form of a genuine appeal and not in fact constitute a weighted or emotionally loaded diktat. Failure to do so undermines the right and responsibility of men

---

[13] Anthony Bash, *Ambassadors for Christ: An Exploration of Ambassadorial Language in the New Testament* (J.C.B.Mohr, Tubingen 1997) 161, 163.

[14] 'Wisdom and Weakness in Ministerial Formation: "Ambassadors" as a Paradigm for the Early Church' to be published in *Power and the Church* (Cassell, London 1997) by Martyn Percy.

and women to choose freely and subverts their God-given capacity to do so.

Third, history teaches us that Christian ministers have experienced enormous difficulty in exercising power Christianity. Paraenetic appeal all too often gives way to authoritarian abuse. Not only are frequent personal reflection and self-examination essential but also rigorous supervision by those unconnected with the minister's own situation.

Although Paul's culture and circumstances were very different from ours, nonetheless he still provides a very powerful model for ministry, particularly for leaders handling power today.

5. The ultimate model

Jesus is the ultimate model. This truth is self-evident – yet how difficult it sometimes is to live out the self-evident. Time and again ministers, unconsciously no doubt, pattern their ministry more on the latest leadership manual than on Jesus himself. What a difference it would make if Christian leaders were constantly evaluating themselves and their ministry in the light of the example of Jesus!

No Christian preacher would question that we need to 'look to Jesus', but to what extent is Hebrews 12:1–3 actually lived out in Christian ministry? In these verses the writer evokes the patience with which Jesus endured opposition and persecution 'for the joy that was set before him'; the emphasis is not on success but on costly faithfulness. The sad truth is that we want to see the power of Christ's resurrection displayed in our lives and in our churches, but we do not want to share in Christ's sufferings. In the perceptive words of Deans Buchanan: 'Rather than allow it to disturb us, we trade in the persecution model for the power model. Seduced by the drive for success, Christian servants adopt triumphalistic patterns of service.'[15]

---

[15] Deans Buchanan, 'Ministry and Suffering in the Life of Paul', *Ministry Today* 8 (October 1996) 6.

Needless to say, costly faithfulness does not necessitate apparent failure. The pursuit of church growth, for instance, which is motivated by a concern for the 'lost' as distinct from a desire for personal or institutional aggrandizement, is not wrong, but commendable. Jesus too was concerned for the 'harvest' (Matt. 9:37,38; John 4:35). There is every reason to rejoice and to thank God when our churches grow as a result of men and women being won to Christ and his church. However, from an eschatological perspective 'success' cannot be measured purely in terms of numbers. Indeed, success cannot be measured upon any external basis. Successful pastoral ministry also encompasses growth and development within the lives of individuals and congregations, as well as within the life of the pastor him/her self! Successful pastoral ministry involves costly faithfulness, which in turn involves modelling ourselves on Jesus.

Jesus is our model. As Jesus himself said, 'A disciple is not above the teacher, but everyone who is fully qualified will be like the teacher' (Lk. 6:40). It is surely significant that the only occasion that Jesus explicitly told his disciples to follow his example was when he washed their feet (John 13:15). Yet to what extent is John 13 with its story of the foot-washing lived out in Christian ministry? There is much to be said for the practice of one North American church, where the pastor at his induction was presented with a towel as a 'sign' of his authority. By contrast, in Britain ordinands at their ordination services are often presented with a Bible as a sign of authority. In one sense that is absolutely right. The Bible is surely our ultimate authority in all matters of faith and practice. And yet as the term 'Bible-basher' reminds, the Bible can be used to bash others, whereas the towel is only of use for service. Maybe at the very least we need to present ordinands with both Bibles and towels!

So it is to the model of Jesus that we now turn. In him we see power incarnate. In him we discover a new dimension to the handling of power.

Chapter Six

Power Incarnate:
Learning from the Life of Jesus

The biggest issue Jesus had to face in his life was the issue of power. For Jesus was by any reckoning a powerful man. Time and again we are told that he taught with an unparalleled sense of 'authority' (e.g. Matt. 7:29; Mark 1:22,27). The miracles he performed were in a very real sense acts of 'power' (*dunameis*: see e.g. Matt. 11:20–24; 13:58; Luke 19:37). Not surprisingly the crowds flocked to listen to him, to see him in action. Here was a leader to follow. In twentieth-century terms, Jesus would have had no difficulty in heading up some mega-church, plus a host of satellite churches.

Yet power, even used for God's sake, was not to be the dominating factor of his ministry. Love was to be his controlling passion, love which never forces itself on another, which always respects the individual and which therefore allows individuals freedom to choose which way they wish to go. All this can be seen clearly in Jesus' wilderness temptations. For the temptations were not just concerned with Jesus' understanding of himself and of his ministry, the desert experience was also a time when Jesus was tempted to misuse his power.

1. Jesus – the man for others

The temptations follow immediately after the baptism of Jesus. In his baptism Jesus had publicly identified himself with the people whom he had come to save. In the waters of the Jordan Jesus had, in the words of the prophet, been 'numbered with the transgressors' (Isa. 53:12) and had thus taken the first step towards the cross. The voice from heaven had acknowledged and confirmed the step Jesus had taken. But what in practice did it mean? What shape was his ministry to take? How was he to use his God-given power?

In this connection the words of Fred Craddock are instructive:

> It is important to keep in mind that a real temptation beckons us to do that about which much good can be said. Stones to bread – the hungry hope so. Take political control – the oppressed hope so. Leap from the temple – those who long for proof of God's power among us hope so. All this is to say that a real temptation is an offer not to fall but to rise. The tempter in Eden did not ask, 'Do you wish to be as the devil?' but 'Do you wish to be as God?'[1]

1.1 The first temptation to misuse power

Matthew and Luke introduce the first temptation to turn stones into bread by saying that Jesus had been fasting for forty days 'and when they were over he was famished' (Luke 4:2). At this point Satan implanted the thought: 'Why not turn stones into bread?' (Matt. 4:3; Luke 4:3). However, the temptation appears to have gone beyond the use of Jesus' power to satisfy his personal needs. It is not far-fetched to suggest that as Jesus contemplated his future ministry, he was tempted to win others by social programmes of one kind or another. He was not the only hungry person in first-century Palestine. Should he not attend to their needs and thus gain their affection? Not only would he win them over to his side, he could so easily sweep them all into the kingdom! This would surely have been a good way to use power for God's sake?

What made such a temptation especially 'diabolical' was that Jesus was being attacked through his love for others: 'In the name

---

[1] Fred Craddock, *Luke – Interpretation Bible Commentary* (John Knox Press, Louisville 1990) 56.

of your Father's compassion for the poor and the hungry, make the stones bread.' Possibly too he was being tempted to prove himself to be the Messiah by a display of divine power, for a repetition of the miracle of the manna in the wilderness was expected to be one of the signs of the coming Messianic age.

Jesus found strength to resist the temptation in the words of Deuteronomy 8:3: 'One shall not live by bread alone.' He recognized that people's hearts hold a deeper hunger than physical need; an appetite more insistent than hunger for bread; a hunger which cannot be satisfied either with bread, or riches, or material comforts. The hunger of men and women for God could be satisfied only as he offered up his broken body on the cross.

Our situation today is very different. In Britain at least we are unlikely to sweep crowds of people into our churches through social programmes or community involvement. Generally speaking, churches which are involved in social action or social service are involved because of the very real needs they see in their communities. Such involvement is right and proper. It is rooted both in Christian compassion, and also in the theological conviction that Kingdom preaching must be accompanied by Kingdom action if it is to be true to the pattern of Jesus (see Matt. 11:2–6).

Yet leaders misuse their power if they allow most – let alone all – of the energies of the church to be channelled into social action as distinct from evangelism. Of course there is a place for meeting people's physical needs, as Jesus recognized when he fed the five thousand. Jesus exercised a holistic ministry. But this holistic ministry involved a recognition that people have spiritual as well as physical and emotional needs. However successful church programmes may be, if they are not meeting people's deepest needs, then ultimately they have failed. One of the significant features of the present time is that, in the Western world at least, people's spiritual needs are coming to the fore. The postmodern age is not a secular age, but rather an age of new religiosity. Ministers and churches must resist the temptation to major on social needs alone – for this generation, as indeed the next, needs also to hear the story of God's love.

1.2 A second temptation to misuse power

If we follow Luke's order (4:5–7; see Matt. 4:8–9), in the second temptation, Jesus found himself on 'a high place' from which he could see 'all the kingdoms of the world' and was tempted to win the world for God by compromising his calling. The temptation here was not literally to bow down and worship Satan. Rather it would appear that Jesus was tempted to renounce the way of the cross by going the easier way of being a political messiah.

The devilish aspect of this temptation was that Jesus' mission was to achieve world-wide dominion. But the end never justifies the means.[2] Although at this stage of his ministry Jesus may not have known exactly what the future held for him, already he knew that he was called to follow a path of suffering. Indeed, it is likely that in those forty days he was meditating on the fourth of the so-called Servant Songs (Isaiah 52:13; 53:12) and seeing the implications of this prophecy for his own ministry. Later he came to see even more clearly that the way to glory was through being 'lifted up' on a cross (John 12:31–32: see Isaiah 52:13). As the author of the great Christ-hymn in Philippians (2:6–11) knew, the path culminating in every knee bowing and every tongue confessing Jesus as Lord led through the cross and resurrection.

Jesus rejected the devil's compromise. He refused to seek to win others by doing any sort of deal with the standards of the world. He recalled Deuteronomy 6:13: 'Worship the Lord your God and serve only him.' Jesus knew that only total obedience to God would do. If that was true for him, it must be true for us too.

Because we live in days when church attendance is dwindling, we face the temptation to demand little of people if only they will come to church. Because we live in a consumer-oriented society, preachers are tempted to pander to the wants of their listeners and

---

[2] Christians cannot be Marxist! The means as well as the end must glorify God. Some lines from TS Eliot, *Murder in the Cathedral*, are pertinent: 'The last temptation is the greatest treason, / To do the right deed for the wrong reason.'

thus to major more on John 3:16 rather than on Mark 8:34. It is easier to speak of the need to believe, than of Jesus' call to repent, to take up our cross and follow him. So preachers proclaim Jesus as Saviour – but not always as Lord. But Jesus demands total obedience: he not only offers a new life; he demands a new life-style.

This radical edge to Gospel preaching has been well described by Jim Wallis:

> The first evangelists did not simply ask people what they believed about Jesus; they called upon their listeners to forsake all and to follow him. To embrace his kingdom meant a radical change not only in outlook but in posture, not only in mind but in heart, not only in world view but in behaviour, not only in thoughts but in actions. Conversation for them was more than a changed intellectual position. It was a whole new beginning.[3]

There is no room for compromise in the Christian life: radical discipleship is the demand. We cannot find God on our own terms – we must come to him on his terms. Church leaders and others misuse their position if they water down the radical nature of the demands of Christ.

But is there not another aspect to this temptation which also has particular relevance to church leaders? Jesus not only refused to seek to win others by compromising with the standards of the world, he also refused to seek to win adulation from others by engaging in power games of one kind or another. Although Jesus called people to follow him, he was not solely concerned with a personal following. Jesus' primary concern was the kingdom of God. True, to receive the message of the Kingdom which he preached involved following in his company – but this following was God-centred and not self-centred.

In *Churches that Abuse* (a better title might have been 'Leaders That Abuse'), Ronald Enroth exposes some of the extraordinarily crass shepherding practices found in certain American churches.

---

[3] Jim Wallis, *The Call to Conversion* (UK edition: Lion, Tring, Herts 1982) 6.

But these practices are not restricted to the USA. They can be found wherever a church becomes cult-like. In this respect the checklist drawn up by the Christian-based Spiritual Counterfeits Project in Berkeley, California, is helpful. The features they identify in their 'Twelve Characteristics of a Counterfeit Church/Cult' are typical of situations where leaders set themselves above others:

1. Authoritarian, oppressive leadership; no room for other ideas and independent action
2. Lack of accountability at the top; leaders don't need or want to answer for their actions
3. Pyramid of power; the further from the top, the less power and influence members have
4. Belief that members and their families are inferior to the leader and his circle
5. Belief that the leader is closer to God and can hear him better than the lay people
6. Strong pressure to conform to the manner, dress, speech etc. of those in power
7. Financial needs of the group (or its leaders) placed above those of members' families
8. Pressure to give undue amounts of time to the group, to neglect other responsibilities
9. An 'us-versus-them' mentality; distrust of all other churches/groups/persuasions
10. Narrow doctrines and teachings so unique that only this group has the 'right path'
11. Discouragement of frank and open discussion about the group, its doctrine, or its leaders
12. Ostracism of former members; prejudice against those no longer 'choosing to belong'.[4]

But power games are played in all sorts of guises – and are not to be found only within the more way-out Christian groups. Even

---

[4] Cited by Roland Howard, *The Rise and Fall of the Nine o'clock Service* 153.

within orthodox mainstream Christian churches ministers, for instance, are too often prone to playing similar power games.

Paul Tournier recognizes this: 'There is in us, especially in those whose intentions are of the purist, an excessive and destructive will to power which eludes even the most sincere and honest self-examination'. Tournier goes on to say that part of the difficulty is that some of our members collude in encouraging us to seek power: 'They look upon us as experts, God's mouthpieces, the interpreters of his will . . . Very soon . . . we find ourselves thinking that when they follow our advice they are obeying God, and that when they resist us they are really resisting God.'[5]

But to go the way of Jesus is to turn one's back on power and on success. For seeking power and success is in effect seeking after self. We, like Jesus, are called to deny self and seek first God's kingdom. Church leaders abuse their power if, for instance, they set themselves up on a pedestal of whatever pattern with a view to gaining some kind of following. The spirit to emulate is that of the Apostle Paul: 'We do not proclaim ourselves; we proclaim Jesus Christ as Lord and ourselves as your slaves for Jesus' sake' (2 Cor. 4:5). Sadly, as experience all too often shows, power can blind those who misuse it.

1.3 A third temptation to misuse power

The third temptation takes place on 'a pinnacle of the temple' (Luke 4:9; Matt. 4:5). It has been suggested that this 'pinnacle' may have been the tall tower in the temple from the top of which a priest used to sound a trumpet to announce the first streaks of dawn and thus the time of morning sacrifice. At such a time the temple court would have been crowded with expectant worshippers, all looking to the tower to see the priest who would give the signal. Had Jesus leaped at that moment, there would have been a large audience to witness a sensational miracle.

Once again Jesus, contemplating the future pattern of his ministry, was tempted to avoid the way of suffering and instead

---

[5]   Paul Tournier, *The Violence Inside* (ET: SCM, London 1978) 137.

to seek to win his contemporaries by some display of supernatural power. What will have put the gloss on this devilish temptation was the fact that some at least of the Jews expected the Messiah to give 'signs'. Thus one of the false messiahs of the time (Theudas, mentioned by Luke in Acts 5:36) persuaded people to follow him to the Jordan by claiming that he would with a word divide the waters in two so that they would pass over dry-shod. True, in the first place the Jews were looking for a Messiah who would repeat the miracles of Moses, but there was no reason in principle why Jesus should not have given some other 'proof' of his status as Messiah.

There in the wilderness Jesus was perhaps tempted to do something startling, dramatic, spectacular, which would bring the world to his feet. But he resisted temptation. Deuteronomy 6:16 warned Israel: 'Do not put the Lord your God to the test'. To have 'leaped from the pinnacle' would have shown not trust in God, but an intention of forcing God's hand by challenging him directly. Had Jesus leaped he would no doubt have gained immediate applause, but he would have scarcely saved a soul. People may acclaim something that stirs their imagination, but they are saved only by something that touches their heart.

We may perhaps see a parallel in the so-called 'power evangelism' popularized by John Wimber and practised by many a 'pentecostal' evangelist. For does that form of evangelism not amount to dragooning people into the Kingdom through spectacular means? How might the third temptation relate to the Toronto blessing and some of the wilder excesses of 'charismania'? Is not much falling on the carpet – described as being 'slain in the Spirit' – more a form of manipulation than of anything else?[6]

The lesson of this third temptation is surely that mind-boggling techniques are not to form part of our armoury. It may well happen from time to time that we wish our churches could be engaged in more spectacular ministry. And yet the spectacular does not sit comfortably with the way of the cross. We are in the

---

[6] See Martyn Percy, *Words, Wonders and Power*.

business of evoking responses in the hearts of men and women. This in turn requires a different approach to evangelism – a different approach to ministry. In the final analysis we are calling people to respond to the *love* of God – and not just to supernatural power.

Luke ends his account of the temptation of Jesus with the words: 'When the devil had finished every test, he departed from him until an opportune time' (Luke 4:13). When that opportune time came, we are not told. It may well be that life for Jesus was a constant struggle to go God's way – that life for him consisted, as it were, of a series of wilderness-type confrontations, culminating in the testing of Gethsemane. But one thing is certain: for Jesus temptation was not just a passing phase, a kind of spiritual adolescence, out of which he eventually grew. Temptation was part of an ongoing spiritual battle, which could only intensify.[7] If this was true for Jesus, then how much more for us – not least in this area of the use and abuse of power?

Undoubtedly Jesus was tempted to abuse his power – and, what is more, to abuse it for God's sake. But the point of the Temptation story is that he resisted the temptation. For him the end never justified the means. The models he developed for ministry were quite other; and although they are rooted in ancient society they are still in principle relevant for ministry today.

2. Jesus – the Servant

It seems likely that for Jesus the key model to his ministry was that of the Servant. When his disciples argued about power and position he told them: 'The Son of Man came not to be served but

---

[7] Luke 22:28, where Jesus says to his disciples, 'You are those who have stood by me in my trials', shows that Hans Conzelmann was wrong to regard the ministry of Jesus as a time 'free from Satan' (see Conzelmann, *Theology of St Luke*, Faber & Faber, London, London 1961, 28–29, 80–81). The natural interpretation of Lk. 4:13 is that Satan left Jesus only for a while, not for the whole of his ministry.

to serve, and to give his life as a ransom for many' (Mark 10:45 – see Isa. 53:11f.). It is undoubtedly such thinking which lies behind the incident in the upper room when Jesus washed the feet of his disciples. In doing this Jesus foreshadowed his death and showed himself to be supremely the Servant of the Lord.

It is impossible to overemphasize the menial nature of the foot-washing. For the rabbis, it was a task which could not be required of a Jewish male slave (*Mekh. Exod.* 21.2.82a, based on Lev. 25:39). Washing the feet of another person was seen as a very undignified action, a job reserved for Gentile slaves, as also for wives and children.

Two Jewish stories illustrate this attitude. The mother of Rabbi Ishmael wished to wash his feet on his return from the synagogue, but he would not allow her to perform so demeaning a task; she on her part requested the court of rabbis to rebuke him for not allowing her the honour. Significant also is the inclusion in a Jewish commentary on Genesis 21:14 of a note that when Abraham sent Hagar away he gave her a bill of divorce, and took her shawl and wrapped it around her waist 'that people should know that she was a slave'.

This is the background to John's description of how Jesus 'got up from table, took off his outer robe, and tied a towel around himself. Then he poured water into a basin and began to wash the disciples' feet and to wipe them with the towel that was tied around him' (John 13:4–5). The disciples would have been amazed. We glimpse their astonishment in the Greek of John 13 gives the impression of Peter spluttering in astonishment and incomprehension: literally, 'Lord, *you* – wash *my* feet . . . !' Peter was shocked. Jesus was 'going too far'.

We don't know the circumstances which occasioned Jesus to wash the disciples' feet. It is possible that Jesus was alone with his disciples in the Upper Room, so that there was nobody else present who might be expected to perform such a menial, albeit necessary, task. As far as the disciples were concerned, such a task was certainly beneath them. But not beneath Jesus! Nor was it only Peter's feet that Jesus washed. He washed the feet of all the disciples – including those of Judas Iscariot.

The way John introduces the story is incredibly moving. He begins with the love of Jesus: 'Having loved his own who were in the world, he loved them to the end' (13:1). This theme of love is picked up later on, when Jesus gives his disciples 'a new commandment' to love one another, as he has loved them (vv. 34,35). Love is clearly the very basis of Jesus' ministry. What was true of him should be true of us too.

John introduces the story of the foot-washing by placing Jesus' action in context: 'Jesus, knowing that the Father had given all things into his hands, and that he had come from God and was going to God . . .' (13:3). Jesus is depicted as being supremely aware of who he was, and yet nevertheless washing his disciples' feet. On the other hand, perhaps it was precisely *because* he knew who he was and what God wanted of him, that he was able to do the unthinkable. Being secure in himself and in his God, he did not have to stand on his dignity.

Yet the incident of the foot-washing illustrates more than simply the willingness of Jesus to put status to one side. As we have already said, for Jesus the foot-washing is an anticipation of the Cross. In the Synoptic Gospels it is the breaking of bread and the pouring of wine that symbolize the divine self-giving; in John's Gospel it is the washing of the disciples feet that symbolizes the divine self-giving. Jesus is therefore not just 'a' servant, he is also the Suffering Servant. The service represented by the washing of the feet is infinitely costly.

We must keep all this in mind as we hear Jesus saying to his disciples: 'If I, your Lord and Teacher, have washed your feet, you also ought to wash one another's feet. For I have set you an example, that you also should do as I have done to you' (vv. 14–15). This word is addressed to all disciples of Jesus – all of us, without exception, are called to serve one another. Yet perhaps we may see in this first instance a particular word to those who are called to positions of leadership and teaching in the church. It is precisely those who have positions of honour in the church of God who are called to be servants of the church of God.

Certainly Jesus said as much to his disciples on other occasions: 'Whoever wishes to become great among you must be your servant, and whoever wishes to be first among you must be slave of all' (Mark 10:43–44). What does this mean in practical terms? Surely, at the very least, that there is no place for status or position within the church of God. To speak of a hierarchy within the church is to go against the spirit of Jesus' teaching. There are no VIPs in the church – or if there are, then all may enter the VIP lounge, for every member is 'very important' in the sight of God.

This does not mean there are no differences in function. Jesus himself recognized that some are called to lead. But he also insisted that leaders are servants. It is true that leaders serve the church of God best when they exercise their God-given gifts of leadership; but in doing so they are serving others, and not themselves – not putting themselves above the others, but rather below them. The foot-washing makes it clear that serving others, far from promoting the interests of self, involves promoting the interests of others. Indeed, as with all true discipleship, serving others involves denying self. In leadership, one aspect of such self-denial may be delegation. In delegating tasks to others we are empowering others to exercise the gifts God has given them. Doing this may not always be easy, especially where the tasks involved are ones we enjoy and feel good in doing. Yet for the sake of the other, as indeed for the sake of the Kingdom, delegation is right and proper. On the other hand, not all delegation is right and proper. There are some tasks which cannot and should not be delegated. In particular, the task of leadership cannot be delegated to others. Formulating the vision and maintaining it are tasks which belong to leadership. The responsibilities of leadership can be heavy and costly and some-times it is tempting to avoid them. In addition, leaders are less likely to be struck by brick-bats if they hide behind others. But leadership patterned on the Servant-King inevitably runs the risk of being unpopular and misunderstood from time to time. It happened to Jesus.

However, leadership patterned on the ministry of Jesus as exemplified in the foot-washing can never be about consolidating personal power. As love for others was the basis for the ministry of Jesus, so love must be the basis of servant-leadership too. The well-being of others always comes first.

3. Jesus the Shepherd

Another model for ministry adopted by Jesus is that of the shepherd. In doing this Jesus took up familiar Old Testament imagery expressing God's love and concern for his people (see, e.g., Ezek. 34). In the parable of the Lost Sheep (Matt.18:12–13; Luke 15:4–7) Jesus by implication likened himself to the shepherd who goes in search of the sheep who has strayed. When challenged by the Canaanite woman, he described himself as being sent '. . . to the lost sheep of the house of Israel' (Matt. 15:24: see also Matt. 10:6). He saw his disciples as God's 'little flock' (Luke 12:32). The same picture was in his mind at the Last Supper when he quoted Zechariah 13:7 ('I will strike the shepherd, and the sheep will be scattered') in connection with the disciples' impending desertion of him (Mark 14:27). He saw himself as a shepherd, not only in relation to his disciples, but to Israel as a whole; Mark describes how on the occasion of the feeding of the five thousand Jesus 'he had compassion for [the crowd], because they were like sheep without a shepherd' (6:34). Matthew says much the same in a more general context: 'When he saw the crowds he had compassion for them, because they were harassed and helpless, like sheep without a shepherd' (Matt. 9:36).

The metaphor is most fully developed in John's Gospel. Two passages are especially significant. In John 10:1–18, Jesus declares; 'I am the good shepherd' (v. 11). At the end of the gospel, in John 21:15–19, the risen Christ commissions Peter to feed his sheep. Indeed, it is because of John 21 that we are able to use John 10 as a pattern for later Christian ministry. In John 10 Jesus does not refer to future leaders acting as shepherds, but John 21 implies an ongoing responsibility. This is presumably why the Anglican ordination service prescribes John 10 as its Gospel reading.

What does the metaphor of the shepherd have to say about the use of power in the church today and about the way in which Christian leadership should be exercised?.

3.1 Relationships

In the first place the metaphor suggests that Christian leadership functions within the context of meaningful relationships. Leadership which is based on the pattern of Jesus does not operate on some kind of impersonal basis from afar. Leadership involves relationships, in which leaders relate with people, and people with leaders.

All this is suggested in the emphasis Jesus puts on the fact that the Good Shepherd knows his sheep: 'He calls his own sheep by name and leads them out . . . and the sheep follow because they know his voice' (vv. 3,4). A little later Jesus repeats the same thought: 'I am the good shepherd. I know my own and my own know me, just as the Father knows me and I know the Father' (vv. 14,15).

This knowledge is experiential and involves an intimate relationship. For whereas 'in the Greek tradition knowledge is thought of as analogous to seeing, with a view to grasping the nature of an object; for the Hebrew, knowledge means experiencing something. In the area of religion, therefore, knowledge of God for the Greek is primarily contemplation of the divine reality; for the Hebrew it means entering into a relationship with God'.[8] This emphasis on relationship is made clear by the imagery of the shepherd and the sheep.

To fully appreciate this imagery here, we have to remember that in the time of Jesus sheep were kept not for their meat but for their milk and their wool. Today most sheep have only a short life before being sent to the abattoir, but in Palestine the shepherd tended his sheep for many years, getting to know them individually. Similarly, the sheep got to know the shepherd and over a

---

[8] George R. Beasley-Murray, *John – Word Biblical Commentary* (Word, Waco, Texas 1987) 170.

period of time a relationship of trust could develop. It was only on the basis of this relationship that the flock trusted itself to be led by the shepherd.

A fascinating insight into the relationship between the Eastern shepherd and his sheep was offered by G.A. Smith:

> On the boundless Eastern pasture, so different from the narrow meadows and dyked hillsides with which we are familiar, the shepherd is indispensable. With us sheep are often left to themselves; I do not remember to have seen in the East a flock without a shepherd. In such a landscape as Judea, where a day's pasture is thinly scattered over an unfenced tract, covered with delusive paths, still frequented by wild beasts, and rolling into the desert, the man and his character are indispensable. . . .
>
> Sometimes we enjoyed our noonday rest beside one of those Judean wells, to which three or four shepherds come down with their flocks. The flocks mixed with each other, and we wondered how each shepherd would get his own again. But after the watering and the playing were over, the shepherds one by one went up different sides of the valley, and each called out his peculiar call; and the sheep drew out of the crowd to their own shepherd, and the flocks passed as orderly as they came.[9]

There are lessons here for Christian leaders. Christian leadership is always concerned for individuals, and not just for the church at large. Effective Christian leadership can never be simply task-orientated, it must be people-orientated too. Indeed, the task or mission of a voluntary organization such as a church can be achieved only as its members come together as a team to fulfil the agreed goals of the church. But for this working together to happen members must feel valued for themselves, and not just for the work they may achieve. Indeed, it is only as people sense that they are loved and cared for that they will co-operate in seeking to fulfil whatever the task might be.

---

[9] G.A. Smith, *The Historical Geography of the Holy Land* (Collins, London 1966 = 25th edition, Hodder & Stoughton, London 1931) 210–211.

One sign that leaders care for people is that they 'know them by name'. They know their individual circumstances. To know people's names is to show that they count. Not to know a person's name is a sign that we do not really care – that they do not really have value. In smaller churches this may be no problem. In larger churches, where visitors may often be present, this may pose a challenge. But how would we feel if God did not know us 'by name'? Those who play power games end up treating people as pawns who can be moved around the board at will; but Jesus – and those who follow in his footsteps – treated people as people, whose concerns are more important than any church programme. One sign that people count is the fact that they are known as individuals.

It is surely significant that not only does the shepherd know the sheep; in addition the sheep know the shepherd. To be meaningful a relationship must be mutual. Leaders do not have to be perfect, but they do have to be seen to be trustworthy. The fact that leaders may be perceived as vulnerable and as frail – like their flock – does not necessarily make them less trustworthy. What counts is that God is seen to be at work in their lives. There is no more place for pretence in Christian leadership, than there is in the Christian life in general. Leadership will be effective not in spite of but because of the fact that leaders are real with their people and that God is seen to be real in leaders' lives. In this sense, Christian leaders who are truly concerned for the welfare of those in their charge have nothing to hide. It is leaders whose motives are questionable and whose eye is on power, who are likely to lose by openness.

3.2 Leading not driving

In the second place, the shepherd metaphor reminds us that true pastoral leadership leads but never drives. It may inspire, but never force. According to Jesus, the good shepherd 'calls his own sheep by name and leads them out. When he has brought out all his own, he goes ahead of them and the sheep follow him because they know his voice' (vv. 3,4). As is well known, in the Middle

East the shepherd goes ahead of the sheep, and the sheep follow. It is only the butcher who drives the sheep! The very metaphor of leadership used here implies the absence of coercion. When Jesus calls, the sheep respond of their own free will. Precisely because they know him, they follow willingly.

There are dangers in drawing too close a parallel between Jesus and ourselves. For Jesus is the 'great shepherd of the sheep' (Heb. 13:20); he is 'the chief shepherd' (1 Pet. 5:4: see 2:25). Today's Christian leaders are at best under-shepherds. We can therefore give a lead only in so far as we ourselves are following the leader. Bishop Lesslie Newbigin once told a group of Indian clergy:

> A true Christian pastor will be one who can dare to say to his people: 'Follow me as I am following Jesus'. That is a terrible test for any pastor. A true pastor must have such a relation with Jesus and with his people, that he follows Jesus and they follow him.[10]

Such a warning should give cause for reflection to some of today's ecclesiastical power-merchants.

That warning apart, we learn here that true Christian leadership can never force others to follow. Leadership is not a form of dictatorship. Leadership may be authoritative, but it is never authoritarian. Leadership is not lordship. In the words of the Apostle Peter, leaders are not to lord it over those in their charge (1 Pet. 5:3). True, Christians are called to respect those who 'have charge of [them] in the Lord' (1 Thess. 5:12). They are even called to 'obey' their leaders (Heb. 13:17). But at the end of the day they have to be given the freedom to choose whether or not they will follow the lead that is being given to them. Power may manipulate, but love always gives choice.

3.3 Seeking the welfare of others

The Good Shepherd of John 10 serves the sheep in his charge, seeking not his own good but theirs. Unlike the 'thief' who 'comes

---

[10] Lesslie Newbigin, *The Good Shepherd* (Mowbray, Oxford 1977) 14.

only to steal and kill and destroy', the good shepherd comes not to deprive people of life, but 'that they may have life, and have it abundantly' (v. 10). What signifies and ultimately sets the seal on his service is the fact that 'the good shepherd lays down his life for the sheep' (v. 11). Whereas the 'hired hand' is only in the shepherding business for what he can get out of it and does not truly care for the sheep (v. 13), Jesus, the Good Shepherd, is not only prepared to give his all for the sheep but actually does 'lay down his life' for them.

In order for the remarkable nature of this service to emerge, we need to rid ourselves of some romantic and sentimental notions concerning sheep. Sheep are not particularly loveable creatures. They can be dirty and pest-ridden. They can be silly and stupid. Yet, in spite of all this, the good shepherd cares for them unreservedly – even if it is to his own detriment.

Again, the lessons are clear. True Christian leadership always enhances the life of others, whereas the abuse of power always leads to the destruction of others. True Christian leadership refuses to use others – whether they be individuals or churches – as stepping stones in a career. Far from living off others, it gives sacrificially to others. And, in the last resort, it is this willingness to lay down one's life for others which ultimately distinguishes a good shepherd from a bad or faithless one. Important as are such things as competence and ability, even more important is love and sacrifice.

3.4 Promoting growth

Shepherding involves making sure that the sheep are fed. After saying that 'whoever enters by me will be saved' Jesus promised that the sheep would 'come in and go out and find pasture' (v. 9). This aspect of the metaphor is not developed in John 10. But it formed a major thrust of Jesus' lakeside conversation with Peter, when Jesus commissioned him to 'feed' both his lambs and his sheep (John 21:15–17). The Good Shepherd is concerned not just for the survival of his sheep, but also for their growth.

Here is another challenge from the 'shepherd' metaphor. Pastoral leadership necessarily includes ensuring the growth of those who are in our care. In Pauls words, it is about 'warning and teaching everyone in all wisdom, so that we may present everyone mature in Christ' (Col. 1:28). Pastoral care is more than seeing to the casualties of life, it is about encouraging personal change and growth of all (Eph. 4:11–16).

So how does a shepherd feed his sheep? Unless the animal is new-born or sickly, the shepherd does not normally bottle-feed it. Good shepherding means leading the sheep into good grazing ground. 'He makes me lie down in green pastures; and he leads me beside still waters' (Ps. 23:2). It is surely not reading too much into the metaphor to suggest that in today's terms feeding the flock does not mean 'spoon-feeding' so much as helping God's people to feed themselves. Christian nurture should not consist in giving detailed instructions about what people must believe or how they must live their lives. It should involve opening up God's Word in such a way that people can discover God's truth for themselves and through appropriate reflection discern how to apply it to their own lives. Good shepherding enables God's people to become mature in their thinking (1 Cor. 14:20). True Christian leadership is not about mind or thought control, but rather about opening up people's minds to God's Word.

In turn this implies that good shepherding encourages diversity rather than uniformity. 'We are . . . to coax different seeds of growth in the people we care for, until they reach a maturity, that richness of character, their own particular character and no one else's.'[11] Where power is exercised aright in the church, there are no clones. People are empowered to become themselves.

3.5 A costly calling

Pastoral leadership can be costly. Unlike the hired hand, who, when he sees the wolf coming, 'leaves the sheep and runs away – and the wolf snatches them and scatters them' (John 10:12), the good shepherd stays at his post, even if this involves the cost of his own life. The good shepherd is not motivated by self-interest,

---

[11] Frank Wright, *Pastoral Care Revisited* (SCM, London 1996) 26.

whether in the form of a wage-packet or of self-preservation, but rather by concern for the sheep. As we have already seen, in true pastoral care the welfare of those in one's charge comes first. At this point, however, the emphasis seems to be on the cost of that caring.

Although the setting is very different, pastoral leadership today can be costly. What we have in mind is not the relatively low salary levels which are the lot of many ministers, but rather the sacrifices of time and energy which are expended in pastoral care. Sometimes there is also the cost of 'stickability' – remaining at one's post in spite of calls to go elsewhere. When things are tough the invitation to accept a 'call' to a bigger and larger church – or indeed, simply to a different church – can be remarkably tempting. But if a church is to grow and to develop, then pastoral longevity is often called for. Short-term pastorates may help ministerial career development, but they may not necessarily help the church. As a rule of thumb, truly productive ministry tends to develop only after a minister has stayed in post for five years or more. In this respect some observations of George Barna are salutary:

> The smaller the church body the more likely the pastor is to spend a few years in that pulpit. Perhaps this is one of the ramifications of the numbers-crazed, upwardly mobile mentality that plagues the pastorate. Failing to accomplish the numerical growth with which the profession is enamored, pastors move to other congregations in hopes of finding a setting more responsive to their efforts. . . . The revolving door syndrome begs the question of whether God really calls most pastors to spend only a few years in each church before moving to new (and presumably greener) pastures.[12]

3.6 A broader horizon

Pastoral leadership which is true to the heart of Jesus will never allow itself to be bound by the church and its needs. The good shepherd is concerned for the sheep which are lost. 'I have other

---

[12] Barna, *Today's Pastors* 37.

sheep that do not belong to this fold. I must bring them also, and they will listen to my voice' (John 10:16). Indeed, if we may judge by the parable of the Shepherd and the Lost Sheep (Matt. 18:12,13), then the lost always have priority over the others. When Jesus was facing criticism he told his critics 'I have come to call not the righteous, but sinners' (Mark 2:17: see also Luke 19:10). The love of Jesus was never exclusive, it was always all-inclusive.

What does this mean in terms of the Christian church today? It means in the first place that no leader with a shepherd's heart can ever be 'owned' by a church. No pastor worthy of the name will become a chaplain figure, simply there to supply the pastoral needs of the church and its members. Concern for the lost and the strayed must always dominate. Mission must always come first on the church's agenda. A church which ceases to live for others ceases to live for Jesus.

Secondly, this particular application of the metaphor emphasizes how seriously harmful power games can be. Where a church is involved in power games, time and again its mission is downgraded and obstructed. In such a situation it is frighteningly easy for the energies of the church to be directed exclusively to internal concerns. Maintenance rather than mission heads the church agenda.

Even more seriously, where there are power games, there are always casualties. The casualties I have in mind are not those who simply transfer from one church to another – although their hurt should not be underestimated – but rather those who give up on the institutional church altogether. They may not give up on God, but they certainly can and do give up on the people of God. Sadly, the quality of the church's life, far from attracting people to the Christian faith and then confirming them in their faith, can prove destructive.

4. Learning from Jesus

Recent years have seen all kinds of major changes taking place in Britain's theological colleges, not least with regard to the area of practical theology. Thirty years ago, for instance, 'pastoralia' often consisted of the college principal simply giving 'tips' from his own somewhat dated experience of church life. Today theological colleges employ a wide range of specialists to teach their students the practical skills of ministry. The contribution of specialist teachers is supplemented by an abundance of specialist books on 'How to be an effective minister'. To be fair, one can learn a great deal from these books and from their authors. However, at the end of the day the essential model for ministry has not changed. Jesus remains the one to whom we should look (Heb. 12:2). He remains the pattern for ministry – even in this admittedly complicated area of power in the church.

Chapter Seven

Power for the People:
Handling Power with Care

From models of ministry we now turn more specifically to some of the practicalities of handling power – and relating to people. How precisely is power to be handled? What does it mean to handle people with care?

1. Power can be good

In the first place, we need to recognize that power is not necessarily evil. Power can be good. Everything depends on how it is handled. Nuclear power for instance, when properly handled, provides light and energy; but it is capable of destroying life and spreading devastation over vast areas.

The Scottish theologian James Mackay helpfully compares power with light:

> Just as the refraction of light reveals the colours in the rainbow, the analysis of power proves it to be deployed along a range of appearances of which raw force is one extreme and pure authority another, and shades composed of mixtures of these in various proportions take up the middle space.[1]

---

[1] James P. Mackey, *Power and Christian Ethics* (Cambridge University Press, Cambridge 1994) 13.

In other words we cannot compare and contrast power with authority, as if the two were antithetical. Authority is but one aspect of power.

Unfortunately many Christians regard power as intrinsically evil. They regard it as a force which is beyond redemption, and which certainly has no business in the church. Martin Hengel, the German New Testament scholar, begins his authoritative work *Christ and Power* with a quotation from Jacob Burckhardt:

> . . . power is of its nature evil, whoever wields it. It is not stability but lust, and 'ipso facto' insatiable, therefore unhappy in itself and doomed to make others unhappy.[2]

Similarly Leith Anderson, the senior pastor of Woodhead Community Church, an American 'mega-church', has likened power to holding a gun to a person's head or withholding a pay-cheque from an employee. 'Power forces others to obey, even against their wills.' He is not alone in contrasting coercive power with legitimate authority:

> Authority is earned. Authority is freely given. Authority is people listening to and acting on the words of a leader because they choose to and want to. Authority is trust and confidence. Not understanding the difference and assuming authority that has not been given is a certain route to disaster in a church or an organization.[3]

Certainly our survey has revealed a good deal of ambivalence towards power among church leaders. It was, for instance, only a bare majority of ministers and church officials who thought that 'power is not a dirty word'.

But such a negative valuation of power is not helpful. Denying the validity of 'power' gets us nowhere – as if power were always a force for evil! The fact is that power of and in itself is morally

---

[2] Cited by Martin Hengel, *Christ and Power* (Christian Journals, Belfast & Dublin 1977) 1,2.

[3] Leith Anderson, *Dying for Change* (Bethany House, Minneapolis 1990) 191.

neutral. Although power can be extraordinarily destructive, it can also be extraordinarily creative. Power can destroy relationships, but it can also restore relationships. Power can oppress, but can also liberate. Power can exploit, but power can also enable. Everything depends on how it is used.

When God gave humankind power ('dominion') over all the creatures (Gen 1:26) he did not intend power to be used for evil, but rather for good. Although humankind has tended to use this power to the detriment of the creation, the hope is nonetheless expressed in Genesis 1 that power will be used positively.

The act of creation itself shows that power is not intrinsically evil. God through his creative power brought order out of chaos. Through his redemptive power he brought life out of death. Through his Spirit he offers this same power to his people. Paul knew from his own experience that God 'by the power at work within us is able to accomplish abundantly far more than all we can ask or imagine' (Eph. 3:20). There is no reason why, in principle, this power should not be available within the church today.

2. Power to exercise

In the second place, we need to recognize that ministers are called upon to exercise the power that is theirs. Power is given to them for a purpose.

Traditionally ordination has been understood as the church conferring on its ministers the authority to preach the word and to administer the sacraments. In the Anglican ordination service, the bishop gives a copy of the Bible to each one of the newly ordained priests and declares: 'Receive this Book as a sign of the authority which God has given you this day to preach the gospel of Christ and to minister his Holy Sacraments' (*ASB*).

Such authority is a form of power. It is the prayer of the church that this power will be used aright. In the words of one of the Anglican ordination collects, the church prays that the newly ordained 'may be found faithful in the ministry they have received'. Faithfulness is present where the preaching of the word and the presiding at the table both point to the Christ who is present in word and sacrament.

Faithfulness in ministry, however, is not to be equated with allowing forms of preaching and worship to become fossilized. In today's post-Christian society there is an urgent need for ministers of the Gospel to use their power more creatively. To preach the gospel of Christ today may involve traditional expository preaching – but it may also involve presenting Christ through the medium of 'seeker services' and the like. To lead the people of God in worship may involve traditional hymns, but it may also involve celebrating the faith through electronic images and synthesized sounds. If today's church leaders are to speak with authority, then they must not only be heard, but also understood. Moth-balled authority has no power as far as the world is concerned.

The authority of the minister is not, however, to be limited to the Word and the Sacraments. Indeed, from a New Testament perspective this priestly emphasis on the role of the minister is misplaced. The New Testament emphasis is upon leadership. Paul, for instance, in 1 Corinthians 12 and Romans 12, as also in Ephesians 4, describes how all God's people are called to serve, but some are called to lead (see Rom. 12:8; 1 Cor. 12:8; Eph. 4:7). It may well be argued that ordination in the New Testament entails the church above all recognizing the authority of its ministers to lead.

Whatever the niceties of theological interpretation as far as ordination is concerned, one thing is certain: if today's churches are to face up today to the challenges offered by contemporary culture, then it desperately needs leaders who will think through those challenges and who will offer strategies for enabling their churches to fulfil Christ's mission today. If such strategies are to be effective, then churches will need leaders who will help enable them to make the necessary changes to their life in order to adopt the necessary strategies.

Today's ministers need to be leaders. Indeed, the respondents in the survey overwhelmingly recognized that 'Ministers have a

God-given authority to lead.' According to John Finney, a personal description for members of the clergy – as also for all in any leadership position within a church – should look like this:

- Analytical and strategic thinker who can convey vision
- Administrator
- Team builder who gets the best out of others
- Deep personal spirituality
- Able to face conflict and enable change
- Warm personality with a heart for mission[4]

In a very real sense the church today needs not more members, but more leaders.[5] For where the right leaders are not only present, but also exercising their power to lead, there the church will grow and new members will be found. What is more, these new members will not just be Christians 'recycled' as it were from other churches, but converts whose lives have truly been turned around by the Gospel of Christ. But this will only happen as leaders exercise their 'powers' of leadership. Chaplains may have a role to play in hospitals and in prisons – they have, however, no role to play in the church. One reason why many churches are making little impact on their communities is that time and again their ministers have felt trapped by the personal needs and expectations of their members. They have assumed the role of their church's personal chaplain. But there is more to ministry in the local church than caring for the pastoral needs of church people – ministry also involves caring for those without. Ordination to the Christian ministry places a call on ministers to mobilize their people for ministry and mission not only in the church, but also beyond the confines of the church.

---

[4] John Finney, 'Patterns of Ministry' 90 in *Treasure in the Field* (Fount/HarperCollins London 1993) edited by David Gillett & Michael Scott-Joynt.
[5] Paul Beasley-Murray, *Dynamic Leadership* 9.

3. Power in trust

Thirdly, Christian leadership, rightly understood, is not just about the exercise of power, it is about power exercised in trust. The church through the act of ordination gives its ministers responsibility to lead the people of God forward in its worship, fellowship and mission to the world. Such a responsibility inevitably brings with it power. It also brings with it accountability.

It is significant that when the Apostle Paul reminded Timothy of his ordination, he reminded him of the power that God had given him:

> Rekindle the gift of God that is within you through the laying on of my hands; for God did not give us a spirit of cowardice, but rather a spirit of power and of love and of self-discipline (2 Tim. 1:6,7).

However, this power was qualified. For besides power Paul mentioned love and self-discipline. The three gifts of power, love, and self-discipline go together. Power, if it is to be used responsibly in the church, must always be complemented by love and self-discipline:

> Power needs to be directed, guided, shaped by love and good sense. Lacking love, power is dangerous. Lacking power, love is ineffective. A love that is empowered but lacking a sound mind is apt to be wild and fruitless.[6]

The 2 Timothy passage seems to imply that Timothy was being tempted not to use the power with which he had been entrusted. He may have felt a natural reticence which made him vulnerable to the temptation to withdraw from his leadership responsibilities. Oden sees such an attitude in the Parable of the Talents. 'The spirit of timidity is typified by the unprofitable servant who would not take responsibility for having buried his one talent – he buried it

---

[6] Thomas C. Oden, *First And Second Timothy and Titus – Interpretation Commentary* (John Knox Press, Louisville 1989) 32–33.

out of anxiety that it might be misused (Matt. 25:25).'[7] Is it reading too much into Scripture to suggest that there are too many 'Timothys' in church leadership today? – leaders who are afraid to lead.

One of the reasons why some may be afraid to exercise leadership today is that they may not be prepared to pay the cost. Leadership is not easy, for instance, when it involves standing up to 'power-brokers' in the church who resist any change because it threatens their comfort or their security. Nor is leadership easy when it involves confronting wayward, albeit powerful, members of the church, whose lifestyle runs contrary to the way of Christ. Sadly, as Stanley Hauerwas and William Willimon, point out:

> What we call church is often a conspiracy of cordiality. Pastors learn to pacify rather than preach to their Ananias's and Sapphiras. . . . Many 'successful' pastors are happy only because they surrendered so early. They let the congregation know that they judged the success of their ministry purely on the basis of how they were liked in the congregation.[8]

Being a leader can be tough. It is sometimes difficult not to be afraid of one's congregation. But failing to exercise one's God-given leadership responsibilities is in fact a misuse of one's calling. Leaders are called to lead. This means that choosing not to lead is actually an abuse of power.

Needless to say, there are inevitable limitations on the power of leaders in the church. For, as the respondents in the survey rightly answered, 'pastoral leadership is non-coercive'. Leadership, if it is truly pastoral, can never 'lord it' over others (1 Peter 5:3). People must always be free to accept or not to accept the direction offered by their leaders. But this does not mean to say that direction is not to be offered. And in the offer of that direction power is inevitably exercised. Walter Wink points out perceptively that although Jesus said, 'Whoever wants to be first

---

[7] *Oden* 33.

[8] Stanley Hauerwas and William Willimon, *Resident Aliens* (Abingdon, Nashville, 1989) 138,141.

must be last of all and servant of all' (Luke 22:24–27), nevertheless Jesus 'does not reject power, but only its use to dominate others'.[9]

Such leadership is always held in trust. It is held in trust, in the sense that leaders are accountable to others. In the first instance, leaders are accountable to God: the day will come when they will have to give an account of their stewardship of 'power' (Heb. 13:17). Not only 'bishops' (Titus 1:7 KJV) but leaders in general are 'stewards of God's mysteries' (1 Cor. 4:1), and in that role they are 'managing' the 'household of God' for their heavenly Master (see Luke 12:42).

But leaders are also accountable to the church. Just as Paul and Barnabas gave an account of their missionary activities to the church at Antioch which had set them apart for this particular work (Acts 13:1–3; 14:27), so today's Christian leaders should be prepared to give an account of their ministry to the people of God. Leaders are not to be a law to themselves. Christ alone is the head of the Body. Rightly understood, the church, in appointing its leaders, has delegated authority to them, authority which the leaders are free to exercise until such time as the church may withdraw its recognition.

4. Checks on power

This accountability of leaders to the church is an important check on their power. It is when such checks are lacking that things can go wrong, with power being misused and in turn people abused. The fact is that leaders are not infallible. Their judgment, like that of any other group of people, can become clouded. Wrong decisions can be made and wrong behaviour ensue. The Apostle Peter, for example, got it wrong when he visited the church in Antioch (Gal. 2:11–14). Paul's instructions for handling accusations against elders (1 Tim. 5:19,20) indicate that local church leaders can get it wrong too.

---

[9]　Walter Wink, *Engaging the Powers* 111.

This accountability of leaders to the church should not be regarded as a restriction, but as a safeguard. The account of the Council of Jerusalem in Acts 15 makes it clear that the lead was taken by James together with the apostles and the elders; but the final decision was made by the church.

In this respect it is significant that both Jesus and Paul stipulate that as and when discipline has to be exercised, this is done not through a single church leader, but through the local church collectively (Matt. 18:15–20; 1 Cor. 5:4,5,13). The ultimate authority is to be found as the church comes together to seek to discern the mind of Christ (Matt. 18:19,20).

But how does this accountability work out in practice? In the average church this is an area requiring a good deal more attention than it usually gets. As we have seen, in most churches account-ability is a myth. Frequently ministers have no job specification and no form of annual review and appraisal. Many church officials, as indeed many churches generally, have little idea about – let alone control over – the way their ministers operate. Such a situation is ripe for exploitation. Precisely because of the fallen-ness of humanity, it is essential to build structural checks into the ministry of the church.

This will involve drawing up a job specification, agreed be-tween the minister and the church, and subject to occasional review. Both the minister and the church will benefit from a clear understanding of the minister's role.

It should also involve an annual appraisal, in which the past twelve months are reviewed and then clear goals set for the future twelve months. The precise mechanics of the annual appraisal will vary from church to church, and from denomination to denomi-nation. However, it is vital that the appraisal takes place at least annually – indeed, there is much to be said for scheduling an interim meeting (say after six months) to monitor progress. Min-isters must be prepared to give up some of their traditional independence and submit themselves to such procedures; without them they are in danger of allowing their freedom to turn into licence, which in turn can encourage power abuse in one form or another.

5. The power of love

A more subjective way of checking the possible misuse of power is for leaders to reflect on what motivates them to seek and to exercise power in the church.

Obviously power for power's sake is wrong; but power for love's sake may be another matter. The difference between using and misusing power has its roots in the motives which underlie the actions. Power combined with self-interest inevitably results in abuse. But 2 Timothy 1:7 links the gift of power with the gift of agape love, which by definition is self-sacrificing, seeking only the good of the other.

Sadly, the power of love is sometimes confused with the love of power. Tom Smail, at one stage a leading figure in charismatic renewal, understands this:

> My own experience of charismatic renewal strongly suggests that if some of its leaders were as concerned with being men of love as they are with being men of power, because they saw that the only power the Spirit has is the power of love, it would be a more wholesome thing than it has sometimes been.[10]

Martyn Percy similarly contrasts the pursuit for power on the part of John Wimber and other charismatic Christians with the biblical affirmation that God is love: 'Wimber puts God's love in the service of his power. Orthodoxy would insist that they should be reversed.' He goes on to point out that the miracles of Jesus are not primarily acts of power, but acts of love:

> The healing miracles of Christ were often his particular response of love to needy individuals . . . Where physical healing does take place, it is often for individuals who are shunned by the prevailing religious institutions, or on the fringes of society. . . . Jesus seldom healed friends.[11]

---

[10] Tom Smail, 'The Love of Power and the Power of Love' *Anvil* 6 (1989) 229.

[11] Martyn Percy, *Words, Wonders and Power* 144.

The miracles of Jesus are clearly more than acts of power, they are acts of powerful love. The underlying motivation must therefore always be one of the key factors in our evaluation of the use of power.

But . . . if only ministers were always clear about their motivation! Unfortunately ministers, like other people can lack self-awareness. Most, if not all, of them would say that they act out of love – but this does not mean that they necessarily do so. We can so easily deceive ourselves – even in those times of quiet when with the best of intentions we may seek to scrutinize our motives before the Lord. We need help from outside to see ourselves as we really are.

It is precisely because motives can all too easily be hidden and unknown that ministers would do well to add the more objective check of spiritual direction. Spiritual direction, rightly exercised, brings to the surface one's own feelings and thoughts and in the process can mercilessly expose false motives. At times such direction can be exceedingly painful – precisely because the real 'person' emerges. However, it is only as the inner self is exposed to God's light and love that there is any hope for growth and development in the Christian life.

It is important to stress that spiritual direction should not be an optional extra for those ministers who are interested in 'that kind of thing'. On the contrary, it is a vital necessity for all engaged in ministry. Spiritual direction is essential for pastoral integrity. It is also essential if ministers are not to abuse their power.

Every four to six weeks I meet my spiritual director, with whose help I have developed a particular 'rule' of life, which amongst other things involves the weekly setting aside of most of a morning to pray over a particular passage of Scripture and 'listen' to God speak into my life. Being honest before God is hard work – it can be also humbling to share some of one's resultant thoughts and reflections with one's spiritual director. Time and again one realizes, as Jeremiah did (17:9), how deceitful and devious the heart can be. Frequently our very best motives go hand in hand with less worthy thoughts. Purity of heart is an ideal constantly to be sought(Matt 5:8), although rarely attained. Spiritual direction does not guarantee perfection; it does, however, provide a more objective check upon the inner self.

6. The power of self-control

Paul, in his injunction to Timothy to 'rekindle the gift of God that is within you', appears to link the exercise of power not only with 'love' but also with 'self-control' or 'self-discipline' (2 Tim. 1:6). The word is interesting, not least because of a possible link with one of the beatitudes. When Jesus said: 'Blessed are the meek, for they will inherit the earth' (Matt. 5:5) the Aramaic word he used may have referred back to the Hebrew text of Psalm 37.11, which mentions the *anawim*. This is the ordinary term for the 'poor' and the 'afflicted'. On the other hand the beatitude as we now have it in the Greek text reflects the Septuagint version of Psalm 37.11, where the word used is *praeis*, 'meek'.

In common Greek usage the 'meek' were not weaklings, but rather the strong whose power was under control. Aristotle, for instance, defined the meek person as one who is 'neither too hasty nor too slow-tempered. He does not become angry with those he ought not to, nor fail to become angry with whom he ought'. Meekness by Aristotle's definition is gentleness combined with strength.

In the so-called 'great invitation' of Matthew 11:29, Jesus invited would-be disciples to take his yoke upon themselves and learn from him 'for I am meek and humble in heart'. The call combines the ideas of gentleness and strength. Jesus is inviting others to experience God's love and power as they live their life in fellowship with himself. It was by this 'meekness' and 'gentleness' of Christ that Paul later appealed to the unruly Corinthians for sympathy and obedience (2 Cor. 10:1).

When Jesus rode into Jerusalem on a donkey he pointed to an Old Testament prophecy in which the expected Messiah was described in terms of 'meekness' (Zech. 9.9). The way in which he cleansed the temple showed that Jesus was no weakling; yet as his encounter with the woman caught in adultery showed, he could be gentle. His passions were under control.

In Jesus we see, to use words made popular by Graham Kendrick, both 'meekness and majesty':

> Meekness and majesty, manhood and deity
> in perfect harmony – the man who is God:
> Lord of eternity dwells in humanity,
> kneels in humility and washes our feet.

All this is highly relevant to Christian leaders. Where power and love and self-control are combined, there 'meekness/gentleness' is found. Such a spirit is to characterize the way in which discipline is exercised (Gal. 6:1) as also the way in which opposition is met (2 Tim. 2:25). God does not want spineless leaders: he wants leaders who are able to speak the truth in love, leaders whose lives exhibit the power of self-control.

> The antithesis of the misuse of power is gentleness, which is best seen and understood within the framework of strength. Gentle leaders, pastors, or teachers, do not force their insights and wisdom on the unlearned, nor flaunt their gifts before those in need. They are patient. They take time for those who are slow to understand. They are compassionate with the weak, and share with those in need. Being a gentle pastor, shepherd, leader, or teacher, is never a sign of being weak, but of possessing power clothed in compassion.[12]

The problem is: how can such self-control can be achieved in practice? No minister would question the need to exercise self-control. The challenge is to translate the ideal into reality. Much more is involved than merely defining the concept; one has, for example, to work out its practical implications for ministry. What does it mean to exercise self-control when counselling a person of the opposite sex? In handling confidences? A difficulty most ministers face is that there is – in Britain at least – no code of

---

[12] Harold Bussell, *Unholy Devotion* (Grand Rapids, Zondervan 1983) 70.

conduct for ministry. Unlike any other profession, ministers in most denominations have no code of professional ethics. Yet the way in which ministers should relate to individuals in the church raises all kinds of ethical implications. Likewise there are ethical implications concerning the leadership styles ministers may adopt. 'Conduct unbecoming' of a minister is a concept that needs to be spelt out. With a view to promoting self-control there is much to be said for ministers adopting (or if necessary drawing up) a code of ethics – a 'rule' of ministry – which in turn may afford them a degree of help and objectivity to promoting self-control within their lives.[13]

Another objective aid to developing self-control in ministry is working under 'supervision'. True, the aim of professional 'supervision is far wider than simply encouraging self-control. However, it does enable people to stand back and examine how they have treated their 'clients', and thereby encourages better pastoral care. Supervision involves the setting of proper boundaries and also accounting for one's dealings with people. Supervision would certainly weed out any form of abusive relationship!

7. Power for the people

The New Testament understanding of the church emphasizes not simply the role of leaders, but also the role that individual members have to play. We see this very clearly in 1 Corinthians 12, where Paul develops the picture of the church as a body. God, says Paul, has designed the body which is the church in such a way that the involvement of every person with his or her special gift is necessary for the proper functioning of the community. Every member has a unique role to play. Although there are particular leadership roles given by God to certain individuals, these individuals do not have a monopoly of the Holy Spirit. The gifts of 'wisdom' and of 'knowledge', of 'faith' and of 'prophecy' are not the exclusive preserve of leaders.

---

[13] For examples of codes of ethics see *A Call to Excellence* 33–38.

This theological insight needs to be combined with an understanding of modern organizational systems. The fact is that a sense
of powerlessness is often a potent breeding ground for subsequent
power struggles. By contrast, where people feel empowered to
take a meaningful part in the decision-making processes of their
church, the possibilities of destructive conflict are reduced.

The American Mennonite Ron Kraybill emphasizes that

> ... where there is dirty fighting, someone is feeling powerless. This
> is hard to remember. Cornered people are often intimidating and can
> inflict serious injury. Worse, they mask their powerlessness – from
> themselves as well as others. Nothing suppresses a whimper better
> than a snarl! As a consequence, the root of the problem often lies
> hidden. Anyone close enough to hear the whimper is likely to get
> snarled at. Or bitten.[14]

Kraybill goes on to distinguish helpfully between 'outcome' powerlessness and 'process' powerlessness:

> Outcome powerlessness is found when one's preference is overruled
> or someone else prevails against one's wishes: 'This form of power-
> lessness disappoints, but doesn't embitter. People healthily empow-
> ered in other ways know that no one wins all the time and tolerate
> such disappointments.'

Process powerlessness, however, is much more serious. For process powerlessness is not just about not winning, but about not
even being 'seriously consulted. Or when the process of arriving
at a decision is too hasty, exclusive or unclear for one to feel a
part of things . . . When people complain about outcomes, they
almost always do so because they believe the process was unfair.'

Often the result is antagonism and lack of trust. For people
need to feel valued; they need to know that their opinions have

---

[14] Ron Krabyill, 'Powerlessness' 96 in *Mediation and Facilitation Training Manual: Foundations and Skills for Contructive Conflict Transformation* (3rd edition, Mennonite Conciliation Service, Akron, Pennsylvania
1995) edited by J.Stuzman & C.Schrock-Shenk.

been heard. This does not mean that they therefore expect to get their own way all the time; it does mean that they feel they count. Empowering the people of God is not only a New Testament principle of leadership, it is also just common sense!

In practical terms this means that there have to be (within the church structures) which give people an opportunity to express their views and to know that their views have been heard and taken seriously. Precisely how this is done will vary from church to church. For churches differ greatly in their power structures. In some churches ultimate power resides in the hands of the leaders – whether they be called ministers, bishops, or elders. In other churches it rests with 'translocal' councils – whether they be called synods or conferences. In churches with a tradition of congregational government ultimate power lies in the 'church meeting', where members come together to discern the mind of Christ. Whatever the power structure, it is vital that people have a regular opportunity not only to receive information about the church, but also to make their own comments and suggestions. There is no place for benevolent paternalism – let alone dictatorship – in the church today!

Not only is it an abuse of personhood – it can also be deemed to be an abuse of the Spirit and his gifts!

8. Power for 'people-building'

For Paul the acid test for the use of spiritual gifts, discussed in 1 Corinthians 12–14, is whether or not the exercise of any gift benefits others. 'Let all things be done for building up' (1 Cor. 14:26). The same maxim can be applied to the exercise of leadership, which is also a gift of the Spirit. Power rightly exercised will result in 'people-building' rather than 'people-using.'

To put it another way, leaders exercise their power most effectively by empowering people to exercise their gifts in turn and fulfil the ministries to which God has called them. Elsewhere Paul says explicitly that God gave gifts of leadership in order to 'equip the saints for the work of ministry' (Eph. 4:11,12). Hence, deduces John Mallison, 'leaders stand accountable not for programmes implemented as much as for gifts released into the community of faith and beyond'.[15] Christian leadership is not about keeping power to oneself, but giving power to others. In the words of Jackson Carroll, 'The secret of exercising power is not to hoard one's power or to use it paternalistically, but to learn together to honour each other's gifts and use one's own gift to strengthen and support the other.'[16] In a very real sense the church is called to be 'a community of empowerment'.

Power is never to be exercised with a view to enhancing the standing of the leader. When it is rightly exercised, it always enhances the standing of the other. Jesus denounced the religious leaders of his day, not least because of their concern for status. He warned his disciples not to be like the scribes and Pharisees who 'love to have the places of honour . . . and to be greeted with respect . . . and to be called rabbi' (Matt. 23:6–7). Instead, they were to avoid being called 'Rabbi (Teacher)', 'Father' or 'Master' (Matt. 23:8–10). John Stott paraphrases this: 'We are not to adopt towards any human being in the church, or to allow anybody to adopt towards us, an attitude of helpless dependence, as of a child on his or her father, or of slavish obedience, as of a servant to his or her master, or of critical acquiescence, as a pupil to his or her teacher.'[17] Christian leaders are rather to be servants (Matt. 23:11) who serve their people best by enabling them to fulfil their God-given potential.

In other words, Christian leadership gives power to the people. The respondents to the survey were right in endorsing the exercise of power in the interests of empowering others. Many ministers would find it a salutary exercise to reflect on the extent to which they had been successful in empowering others over the past twelve months! Indeed, one practical check might be to ensure that this aspect of ministry is discussed at every appraisal.

---

[15] John Mallison, *Grid* (Summer 1987).

[16] Jackson W. Carroll, *As One With Authority* (Westminster/John Knox Press, Louisville 1991) 95.

[17] John Stott, *The Contemporary Christian* (IVP, Leicester 1992) 291.

9. Power in weakness

At one stage in the analysis of the survey we identified three different ways in which leaders may exercise power: power from 'above', power from 'within' and power 'with'. Sometimes, however, Christian leaders discover that none of these ways of operating is available to them. Perhaps as a result of some power struggle in the church, all of a sudden they find themselves deprived of their power. They no longer have any influence in the church. Indeed, they may have been summarily expelled from it. At such times there is another form of power available – but in the first instance not power to exercise, but rather power to receive – power 'from below'.

If there is one passage of Scripture which should be written on the heart of every Christian leader it is 2 Corinthians 4:7–12. Paul begins: 'But we have this treasure in clay jars, so that it may be made clear that this extraordinary power belongs to God and does not come from us' (2 Cor. 4:7). There are times in ministry when we become acutely aware of our fragility and frailty, when perhaps it feels as if the 'clay jar' has not just been badly cracked, but irredeemably broken. Yet all is not lost. For human weakness is always an opportunity for God's power to be at work. To borrow from JB Phillips's translation, we may be 'knocked down', but we are not necessarily 'knocked out'. 'Death' need not have the last word; 'resurrection' may be around the corner – not just in the next life, but in this life too. For while we may be weak, God's power is 'extraordinary'.

The theme of power in weakness is picked up a little later in 2 Corinthians 12. At a time of unanswered prayer God so to speak 'breaks through' Paul's 'break-down'. 'My grace is sufficient for you, for power is made perfect in weakness' (2 Cor. 12:9). When Paul came to the end of his own resources, he discovered far greater resources in Christ. In God's topsy-turvy world weakness is a pre-condition for power. Oswald Chambers comments:

> God can achieve his purpose either through the absence of human power and resources, or the abandonment of reliance upon them. All

through history God has chosen and used nobodies, because the unusual dependence upon him made possible the unique display of power and grace. He chose and used somebody only when they renounced dependence on their natural abilities and resources.[18]

We see weakness and power come together supremely in the Cross of Christ. From one point of view, the crucified Christ is a picture of disaster and defeat. 'He saved others; he cannot save himself', said the mockers. Ironically, there was more truth in their statement than they realized. Precisely because he did not save himself he had the power to save others. Christ's apparent weakness became a catalyst for saving power. Paradoxically, Christ's very non-resistance became the means by which he over-powered the Evil One. It was as Jesus divested himself of his power that he disarmed the 'principalities and powers': the Cross became not the scene of defeat, but of triumph (Col. 2:15).

Jesus did not attack evil by standing outside it in divine immunity and smashing it with the laser beams of supernatural force; he did not defeat it by violent and overwhelming assault upon it, but rather by taking it on himself and letting it do its worst to him.[19]

In this respect, the Cross of Christ is not just a one-off event. It is also a paradigm for all Christian people. 'Christ also suffered for you, leaving you an example, so that you should follow in his steps . . . When he was abused, he did not return abuse; when he suffered, he did not threaten; but he entrusted himself to the one who judges justly' (1 Peter 2:21,23). In the first place these words are applicable to all Christians and refer to suffering caused by unbelievers. But I believe we may also apply them to Christians whose suffering is caused by other Christians; even perhaps to Christian leaders abused by other

---

[18] Oswald Chambers, *Leadership* (Summer 1993) 111.
[19] Tom Smail in *Charismatic Renewal: The Search for a Theology* by T.Smail, A.Walker & N.Wright (SPCK, London 1993) 62.

leaders. For sadly Christians can be unspeakably cruel to one another.[20] And although Peter no doubt had vindication beyond the grave in mind, the experience of many is that God uses those moments of suffering and of weakness to become gateways to victory and to power.

10. Power for 'pastor building'

So far the thrust of this chapter has been on the power of ministers to affect the life of the church. However, as we have seen in the survey, power is not simply in the hands of ministers. Power can be exercised apart from ministers by others in the church. What's more, such power can be abusive power, bringing suffering not only to the ministers themselves, but also to their families. In the words of Patricia Fouque:

> Abuse within the church is two-way. Very real abuses are experienced by ministers and leaders, as also by their families. Children of the Manse or Vicarage carry heavy burdens, and when there is conflict in the church or their father is dismissed from post, they have to face not only a change of school, friends, church, but also their parents' pain. Many are left with a deep sense of betrayal and struggle well into adult years, with feelings of bitterness, resentment and anger.[21]

It is therefore not just churches which need to be handled with care, but also pastors and their families. Pastors – and their families – are human. They bleed. They are fallible. And they are Christ's gift to the church (Eph. 4:7). As such they should be handled not only with care, but also with respect.

---

[20] See Morris West, *A View from the Ridge* (HarperCollins 1996) 8: 'What I cannot forgive, and what I can never condone, is the impersonal cruelty that institutions – my own church among them – practice upon their members and that they justify by a thousand arguments . . .'. See also Alistair Ross, *Evangelicals in Exile* 98–114.

[21] Patricia Fouque, 'Abuse In Ministry', *Ministry Today* 10 (June 1997) 10.

What does this mean in practical terms? In the first place, church members need to accept their pastoral responsibility for ministers and their families. The pastoral care of ministers and their families is not just the responsibility of outside figures such as bishops and superintendents, but first and foremost of those whom they seek to serve. One way of giving expression to that responsibility is for leaders once a year to review the general well-being of their pastor – and of the family where appropriate; it should be as much an agenda item as, for instance, in certain churches the annual review of the pastor's salary is an agenda item. Such a forum might well consider issues such as work- overload etc.

Secondly, leaders need to ensure that the financial arrangements for their ministers are fair and God-honouring. These include not only salary and housing (or housing allowance), but also expenses incurred as a result of administration, travel, study, hospitality etc. Penny-pinching can well be tantamount to abuse.

Thirdly, leaders need to encourage their minister to use the services of a spiritual director. As we have seen, spiritual direction is not a luxury, but a necessity. Similarly ministers need to be encouraged to explore forms of supervision. 'Who is to guard the guards themselves? Who is to watch over those who are doing the watching?' When the Roman poet Juvenal wrote these words he was thinking of the enticement of guards by a woman, but they are capable of more general application. Ministers are vulnerable people, and all the more so because of their calling. They need to be 'guarded' and not just helped.

Fourthly, leaders need to ensure that there is a system for annual appraisal and review. If not, then they should take steps to set up such a system. As we have already seen, appraisals give an opportunity for leaders to affirm their pastor and to say 'well done', to review previously set objectives and set future goals, to provide a safe environment for discussing problems and, where necessary, to express dissatisfaction, and to identify needs for further training and development.

Fifthly, when difficulties arise, as inevitably they do, leaders should always be ready to defend their pastor against unfair criticism. Time and again the minister is made the 'scapegoat' when things seem to be going wrong in the church. The 'buck' stops at the minister's office. Not surprisingly the majority of ministers believe that at times they have been unjustly treated by the church, and not least in the area of unfair criticism. Yet even where the criticism is fair, leaders should in the first place speak privately to the pastor, face to face, rather than join in the public criticism. Anything else is abuse.

Sixthly, churches should consider appointing a minister's advocate, who can represent the minister's interests. Such an 'advocate' cannot normally be a church official, since by definition church officials represent the interests of the church. Instead, an independent person of standing should be found. Such an appointment is helpful at any time but especially so when difficulties arise, whether of the pastor's own making or not. In such a situation it is good for the leaders to know that somebody is able to speak on the pastor's behalf and represent the concerns of the pastor. Sadly, experience shows that when things go wrong, churches are not always fair in the way they treat their minister. Nor for that matter are bishops and superintendents necessarily helpful – for they are likely to allow the interests of the institution rather than of the individual to take precedence (see John 11:50)![22]

11. Power abused

What happens when, in spite of best intentions, everything goes wrong and power is grossly abused? When, for reasons good or bad, the minister is forced to leave the church, and pain abounds? As we have already seen, ministerial terminations are not uncommon. At some stage most ministers have the experience of leaving a church in unhappy circumstances.

---

[22] In this regard some words of Morris West are apposite: 'Institutional power distances men and women from their own humanity. They forget that men and women, not institutions, are the subjects and objects of salvation. The institutions may survive; people have only their precarious now' (*A View from the Ridge* 111).

The temptation churches face is to try to forget the whole unseemly incident. To push everything under the carpet and pretend it never happened. To appoint another minister and simply begin another chapter. But life is not that simple. Just as a hasty re-marriage after a painful divorce would be unwise, so too the hasty engagement of another pastor following a 'messy' severance would be an act of folly. For one thing, there are lessons to be learned. Even more important, there is also sin to be dealt with.

In the introduction reference was made to the troubles at Lincoln Cathedral, troubles which in one guise or another have apparently bedevilled the place for centuries. The troubles at Lincoln can be paralleled many times over – there are churches, for instance, where down through the years almost every minister has left under a cloud. There are Christian institutions where the leadership has almost perpetually been dogged by unhappiness, and at times by outright conflict. In such it would appear that there has been some kind of institutional 'virus', evil in nature, which has never been dealt with properly. The cast has changed, but not the plot. A study of involuntary terminations of ministers within three American denominations, concluded that '40% of the Episcopal churches, 34% of the United Churches of Christ, and 45% of the Presbyterian churches had existing conflict or problems in the congregation before the terminated pastor started his or her job'.[23] The implication is that the ministers concerned in such situations were innocent 'lightning rods' who quite unjustly bore the brunt of long-standing factionalism in their churches. In terms of the theological framework developed by Walter Wink, the fallen principalities and powers are having a field day. The weapons that have been used have not been of Christ, and so the demonic element within the structures has emerged unscathed.

The first step in dealing with a situation of power abuse, whatever the form, is for the church to acknowledge its share in the sinfulness of the situation. Just as in the breakdown of relationships within a marriage, there is rarely an innocent party, so too in the

---

[23] Speed Leas, *A Study of Involuntary Terminations in some Presbyterian, Episcopal, and United Church of Christ Congregations* (Alban Institute, Bethesda 1980) 11.

breakdown of relationships within a church. True, one party may be more guilty than another. True, one party may be the 'injured' or 'wronged' party. But sin rarely confines itself to one group within a church. If an abuse of power is not to be repeated, the church needs to face up to its culpability and acknowledge its share of guilt. Such a confession of shared culpability is difficult enough within a secular organization, but within a church it is doubly difficult. For, as we have seen, God is brought into the situation and where God is on 'our side', we feel doubly righteous. It takes a good deal of insight and humility for people involved in church fights to acknowledge that they too were in the wrong.

But confession is not enough. Repentance too is necessary. In biblical terms, this entails more than being sorry about the mess. Repentance involves a 'turning around'. Lessons need to be learned, new attitudes need to be adopted, new structures need to be put in place, to ensure that whatever has happened will never happen again. To ensure that such repentance is genuine, the repentance – as also the confession – need to be made public. Changes are not to be brought in by sleight of hand, but with the knowledge of the whole church.

Thirdly, forgiveness needs to be exercised – to be sought as well as to be received . . . Where major hurt has been caused and great wrong has been done, forgiveness is never easy. Where lives have been ravaged, careers halted, faith destroyed, where children have been damaged . . . in situations like these, forgiveness is never easy. Indeed, forgiving can be a battle. Pride, anger, bitterness, resentment – all rise to the surface. Yet forgiveness is at the heart of the Christian faith. 'If you do not forgive others, neither will your Father forgive your trespasses' (Matt. 6:15). Jesus showed very clearly on the cross that there is no sin that is not forgiveable, impossible though forgiveness at times may seem. What's more, just as the cross was God's way of triumphing in Christ over the principalities and powers, so too the cross and all that it stands for must have the last word in power struggles today; without the forgiving power of the cross the world and the church remain in the grip of those principalities and powers. Power struggles will continue to plague the church's life. And the world will be given no reason to believe.

Fourthly, where possible, there needs to be some kind of public expression of reconciliation. For power struggles in the church are never private. The shock waves go through the local community and often further afield too. The shock waves also spread down through the years of the church's future. The cross must be seen to have triumphed – for the sake of the community as well as for the sake of the church's future.

Needless to say, this is a complex process. Almost certainly some kind of outside church 'consultant' will be needed, to help forward the process. Indeed, perhaps the first step in the process is the appointment of such a consultant. Would that in Britain we had the American system of 'interim ministers'. As the name suggests, 'interim ministers' serve a church for a limited period – normally no longer than 12 months – and act as a buffer between the ending of one ministry and the beginning of another. Where there has been a church fight, such interim ministers can help a church to deal with its past. It is neither fair nor right for a new minister to be expected to sort out the problems of the past. Nor for that matter should a church consider appointing a new minister until it has truly been able to put the past to rest.

12. People power

Power for God's sake always has the welfare of people at heart. 'We do not proclaim ourselves', wrote Paul; 'we proclaim Jesus as Lord and ourselves as your slaves for Jesus' sake' (2 Cor. 4:5). Every time it must be people who take precedence over personal and institutional well-being. As Martyn Percy so rightly says in his critique of the Anglican Turnbull report, 'Management and efficiency are not at the "heart" of leadership as portrayed in the New Testament. Instead service and sacrifice are presented as "models", mirroring the kenosis of Christ.'[24] Management and efficiency can so easily become false gods serving the interests of the institution. But power is for people.

---

[24] Martyn Percy, *Power and the Church*.

Some Final Thoughts

Abuse for God's sake? No, no, no! The title for this book was chosen not so much to pose a question, but rather to underline the irony of the situation. Where power is misused, God and his kingdom suffer. People are hurt, faith is undermined, and the Gospel is called into question. Power wrongly used always adversely affects the mission of the church. Where power games are being played, so much energy is misdirected. Individuals and groups in the church become inward-looking rather than outward-looking. The church, and the struggles within the church, become the focus of their attention, rather than the world for whom Christ died. From a human perspective at least, in such a situation God, the church, and the world, are all losers.

One of my aims in writing this book has been to expose the dangerous reality of power in the church. I trust I have done so. True, at first sight there appears, for the most part, to be nothing sensational about the abuse of power among God's people. But herein is to be found the danger. If the abuse of power were rampant in every church, then it would be obvious to most, if not to all. However, it is precisely because the abuse of power is less melodramatic and more subtle that many fail to see the problem. Hopefully the problem has now been exposed.

The problem of abuse of power in the church, however, is compounded by the fact that God is often brought into the issue. This may seem a strange comment, because one might well assume that if God were brought into a problem, then the problem might be solved. And that it true. Where God is brought into a problem and allowed to have his say, as it were, problems do begin to be solved. Sadly, in the church God is often brought in to bolster up our side. Like the German army, whose soldiers once wore belts with the words 'Gott mit uns' (God with us) we tend to want to use God for our own ends, rather than submit to his purposes. The reality is that when we seek to use God for our own ends, not only do we become blinded to the blasphemy of seeking to use God for our own ends, we also become blind to the weaknesses of our own position. Indeed, not only do we become blind, we become even more arrogant and even more resistant to other ways of looking at things, with the result that there is greater intensity to the power-struggle. With God on our side, the inevitable conclusion is that the other side is doing the Devil's work. As history proves, religious conflicts are the worst.

How can this problem of power in the church be effectively addressed? In this book we have sought to explore three avenues.

In the first place we have sought to expose the problem of power in the church. As we have argued, it is the very hiddenness of the abuse of power which makes it all the more dangerous. Once we become aware of the issues surrounding the abuse of power, that moment we become the better able to deal with abusive power when it raises its ugly head. But it is not only awareness that needs to be promoted: self-awareness is also crucial. For the problem does not always lie with others – it sometimes lies with ourselves. As we have seen from the survey, few, if any leaders, can truthfully put their hand on their heart and say they have never abused their position. Abuse is deceptive – not least to the abuser. The fact is that our motives and our actions are not always as pure as they might be – indeed, are they ever? Half the battle against the abuse of power in the church may actually lie in self-awareness.

In the second place, we have sought to address the problem by reflecting on some of the issues surrounding the use of power. We have seen that the exercise of power in itself is not morally wrong, provided that the exercise of such power in Christian service is complemented by love and self-discipline.

In the third place, we have sought to address the problem by learning from Jesus himself. For Jesus is the pattern for our living, and for our leading. As Leighton Ford wrote in his preface to *Jesus: The Transforming Leader*:

> The understanding of Jesus' leadership is not only important, but essential to our time. He was able to create, articulate and communicate a compelling vison; to change what people talk about and dream of; to make his followers transcend self-interest; to enable us to see ourselves and our world in a new way; to provide prophetic insight into the very heart of things, and to bring about the highest order of change.[1]

Jesus too is the pattern for our serving. 'Let the same mind be in you that was in Christ Jesus', wrote Paul to the Philippians, and thereupon cited that great Christ-hymn, which tells of how the Lord Jesus emptied himself of all his rights and privileges in order to serve the purposes of God (Phil, 2:5–11). Jesus reversed all human ideas of greatness and rank, and in so doing unleashed in an unparalleled way the power of God into our world. Power for God's sake is power surrendered in the service of others.

---

[1] Leighton Ford, *Jesus: The Transforming Leader* (London: Hodder & Stoughton, 1991) xv.

Appendix One
(*Ministers*)

Leadership Styles

Classification Data I - The Church
PLEASE TICK BOX OR WRITE IN ANSWER - WHICHEVER IS APPLICABLE

1 Name of Church(es) ....

2 Denomination..

3 Number of Churches for which you have pastoral oversight ....

4 Number on church roll(s) ....

5 Number at typical Sunday morning service(s) ....

6 Social class composition of congregation:

Mainly manual/ working class □ 1	Mainly academic/ professional □ 2	About equally divided between each □ 3

7 Theological position of church (you may tick more than one box)

Fundamentalist □ 1	Middle of the road □ 3	Charismatic □ 5
Evangelical □ 2	Liberal □ 4	Catholic □ 6

Classification Data II - The Minister

8 Name ....

9 Sex:

Male □ 1   Female □ 2

10 Age:

< 30 □ 1	45-54 □ 3	65+ □ 5
31-44 □ 2	55-64 □ 4	

11 Marital Status:

Married □ 1   Single □ 2   Divorced/separated □ 3   Widowed □ 4

If married Does your wife have a regular paid job?   Yes □ 1   No □ 2

12 Length of Time in Ministry ....   _____ years

13 Length of Time in present church...................................   _____ years

14 Length of your predecessor's ministry in this church...............   _____ years

15 Length of interregnum between yourself and your predecessor......   _____ years

16 Security of ministerial tenure:

3 months notice □ 1	9 months notice □ 3	Notice unspecified □ 5
6 months notice □ 2	12 months notice □ 4	Freehold □ 6

17 (a) Are you the:

Sole Minister □ 1	Senior Minister □ 2	Associate/ Assistant Minister/Curate □ 3

(b) How many Assistant/Associate Ministers/Curates do you have? Male.............   Female ....

(c) If senior minister: Did you recruit your assistant(s) or inherit them with the post?

Recruit □ 1   Inherit □ 2

1

18 Do you have a full/part time Church Administrator:
Yes ☐ 1   No ☐ 2

19 Other Church staff WRITE IN: . ...

20 Do you usually work from home, or do you have an office at the church?
Usually work from home ☐ 1   usually work in church office ☐ 2

21 Does your wife have a recognised role in the church?
Yes ☐ 1   No ☐ 2

If yes, what is her particular role? ....

22 What is your own theological position (if different from 7 above)

Fundamentalist	☐ 1	Middle of the road	☐ 3	Charismatic	☐ 5
Evangelical	☐ 2	Liberal	☐ 4	Catholic	☐ 6

23 (a) Please indicate your stipend range (per annum)

Under £10,000	☐ 1	£12,500 - £14,999	☐ 3	£20,000 or more	☐ 5
£10,000-£12,499	☐ 2	£15,000 - £19,999	☐ 4		

(b) Do you live in rent free accommodation?
Yes ☐ 1   No ☐ 2

Classification Data III - Church Growth (Numerical)

24 In terms of numbers, before you arrived as minister, was the church:
growing strongly ☐ 1   growing slowly ☐ 2   holding its own ☐ 3   declining ☐ 4

25 Since your arrival has the church been:
growing strongly ☐ 1   growing slowly ☐ 2   holding its own ☐ 3   declining ☐ 4

26 How do you view future prospects for growth?
excellent ☐ 1   good ☐ 2   fair ☐ 3   poor ☐ 4

27 Do you feel that the church measures your success in terms of growth?
Yes, very much ☐ 1   Yes, to some extent ☐ 2   No, not at all ☐ 3

Ministry I - The Call/Nature of Ministry

1 How satisfied are you with your present ministry?
very satisfied ☐ 1   fairly satisfied ☐ 2   not really satisfied ☐ 3   not at all satisfied ☐ 4

2 Do you still enjoy ministry in general?
very much ☐ 1   quite a lot ☐ 2   not very much ☐ 3   not at all ☐ 4

3 Do you enjoy your present ministry?
very much ☐ 1   quite a lot ☐ 2   not very much ☐ 3   not at all ☐ 4

4 Have you ever thought of moving out of ministry?   Yes ☐ 1   No ☐ 2

If yes, please say why? ....
....
....

If no, why do you stay in ministry? ....
....

5   What about your 'fit' with your present church - Do you share common values?
    totally   ☐ 1   for the most part   ☐ 2   no, not really   ☐ 3   not at all   ☐ 4

	Definitely	To some extent	No
	1	2	3
6 Has pastoring this church increased your passion for ministry?	☐	☐	☐
7 Has pastoring this church been difficult on your family?	☐	☐	☐
8 Would you hope to move on to a larger church?	☐	☐	☐
9 Do you feel you could accomplish more in another church?	☐	☐	☐
10 Do you feel your gifts are being fully used?	☐	☐	☐
11 Do you believe you have the capacity to pastor a bigger church?	☐	☐	☐
12 Would you like (have liked) to be a 'bishop-figure'?	☐	☐	☐

13 How ambitious are you?
    very   fairly   not very   not at all
    ambitious   ☐ 1   ambitious   ☐ 2   ambitious   ☐ 3   ambitious   ☐ 4

14 How has ambition affected your ministry:
    very positively   ☐ 1   neither positively or negatively   ☐ 3   fairly negatively   ☐ 4
    fairly positively   ☐ 2   very negatively   ☐ 5

    Please give an example of positive affect...
    ....

    Please give an example of negative affect ....
    ....

15 How competitive are you?
    very   ☐ 1   quite   ☐ 2   not very   ☐ 3   not at all   ☐ 4

16 If very/quite, with **whom** are you competing?...
    ....

17 What **professional** goals do you have? ....
    ....
    ....

18 What **personal** goals do you have?..
    ....
    ....

19 (a) In an average week, what is the **total** number of hours you work for the church _____ hours

(b) How **many hours** in an average week do you give to each of the following activities (WRITE IN BELOW)

(c) What do you **enjoy** most in ministry? Please give each item listed an enjoyment rating out of 10.
(i.e. 10 = Maximum enjoyment, 0 = minimum enjoyment)

	Q 19(b) Number of Hours	Q 19(c) Rating out of 10
administration		
committees		
community involvement/social action		
counselling		
discipling/nurturing		
enabling/involving the laity in ministry		
evangelism		
prayer and meditation		
sermon preparation/preaching		
study		
visiting - building & maintaining meaningful relationships		
worship preparation/leading worship		

20 What are the major **problems or frustrations** which you encounter in carrying out your task of ministry? Please give each of the following issues a rating out of 10 (THE MORE DIFFICULT THE ISSUE, THE HIGHER THE RATING)

	Rating out of 10
lack of commitment on part of your members	
low level of spiritual maturity of people	
gaining greater involvement by your members	
administration	
how to do effective outreach	
implementing change	
counselling	
developing a sense of community within the congregation	
church politics	
relational difficulties between leaders	
relational difficulties between leaders and the congregation	
relational difficulties among members of the congregation	

Ministry II - Leadership Style

1 Which of the following personality types do you consider yourself to be?
High-key, aggressive   ☐ 1   Low-key, laid-back   ☐ 2

2 Which of the following best describes your leadership style?
autocratic ☐ 1   persuasive   ☐ 2   consultative   ☐ 3   participative ☐ 4

3 (a) Do you more often try to:
help people say what they think   ☐ 1   **or**   do you say what you think right away? ☐ 2

(b) Do you see yourself in the first place as
a manager of a process   ☐ 1   **or**   as a leader of people?   ☐ 2

(c) Do you have a clear sense of vision for the life of your church?
Yes ☐ 1   No ☐ 2

If so, please sum it up in one sentence (if you can!):...
....

4

Ministerial Accountability

1 To whom in **theory** are you accountable? ....

2 To whom in **practise** are you accountable? ....

3 Do you have a formal job description?
   Yes ❑ 1   No ❑ 2

4 Do you undergo regular appraisal?
   Yes ❑ 1   No ❑ 2

5 If so, how often? ....

   By whom? ....

6 Do you meet on a regular basis with any of the following:

	Yes	No		Yes	No
	1	2		1	2
a supervisor	❑	❑	a work consultant	❑	❑
a spiritual director	❑	❑	other (WRITE IN) _____		
a therapist	❑	❑	_____	❑	❑

7a) Has your church developed a 'mission statement'?
   Yes ❑ 1   No ❑ 2

7b) If yes, please state it ....

....

8 To what extent do you see yourself actively fulfilling that mission statement?
   totally ❑ 1   for the most part ❑ 2   not at all ❑ 3

9 In Church meetings to what extent does the "agenda" revolve around issues of mission rather than issues of maintenance (finance, fabric, etc.)?

Totally mission	❑ 1	¼ mission, ¾ maintenance	❑ 4
¾ mission, ¼ maintenance	❑ 2	Totally maintenance	❑ 5
½ mission, ½ maintenance	❑ 3		

The Structure of Power In The Church

1a) Please tick the box which most reflects your agreement/disagreement with these statements.

	Agree Strongly	Agree slightly	Neither Agree nor Disagree	Disagree slightly	Disagree Strongly
	1	2	3	4	5
"God wants us to be powerful because there is a lot God wants us to do"	❑	❑	❑	❑	❑
"Power is not a dirty word. It is the ability to mobilise resources"	❑	❑	❑	❑	❑
"The exercise of power can only be justified in the interests of empowering others"	❑	❑	❑	❑	❑
"Power is like saltwater: the more you drink the thirstier you become"	❑	❑	❑	❑	❑
"Power tends to corrupt, and absolute power corrupts absolutely, and this is especially true of religion"	❑	❑	❑	❑	❑
"Resorting to piety is a power play peculiar to Christians"	❑	❑	❑	❑	❑
"The exercise of power always implies coercion and violence"	❑	❑	❑	❑	❑
"Power is a serious problem in the church today"	❑	❑	❑	❑	❑

1b) Please tick the box which most reflects your agreement/disagreement with these statements.

	Agree Strongly	Agree slightly	Neither Agree nor Disagree	Disagree slightly	Disagree Strongly
	1	2	3	4	5
"Ministers exercise too much power"	☐	☐	☐	☐	☐
"Ministers need to delegate more"	☐	☐	☐	☐	☐
"Ministers need to be people-orientated, not goal-orientated"	☐	☐	☐	☐	☐
"Pastoral leadership is non-coercive"	☐	☐	☐	☐	☐
"Personal growth is more important than church growth"	☐	☐	☐	☐	☐
"Ministers have a God-given authority to lead"	☐	☐	☐	☐	☐
"Churches benefit from strong leadership"	☐	☐	☐	☐	☐
"The key to church growth is leadership"	☐	☐	☐	☐	☐
"Ministers should not be afraid to use their power"	☐	☐	☐	☐	☐
"Good pastoral leadership is directive"	☐	☐	☐	☐	☐

2 How do you mostly tend to exercise power? Is it:

'over' people as you give a strong lead ☐ 1

'within' the church by inspiration of your personality ☐ 2

'with' people as you in turn empower them ☐ 3

3. To what extent have you been involved in doing any of the following?

	Very often	Fairly often	Rarely	Never
	1	2	3	4
imposing your own style of worship	☐	☐	☐	☐
using your sexuality to help you get your own way	☐	☐	☐	☐
being manipulative in church meetings in order to get your own way	☐	☐	☐	☐
not providing a lead when it is needed	☐	☐	☐	☐
pushing through a course of action that was unpopular	☐	☐	☐	☐
playing on the guilt of members of the congregation	☐	☐	☐	☐
'hiding behind God' in order to get your own way	☐	☐	☐	☐
intimidating weaker people into a course of action	☐	☐	☐	☐

4 Please tick the box which in your view best describes the strength of power exerted by each of the following groups of people in your church:

	Very strong	Strong	Neither Strong nor Weak	Weak	Very Weak
	1	2	3	4	5
Congregation/Church meeting	☐	☐	☐	☐	☐
Elders/Deacons/PCC	☐	☐	☐	☐	☐
Former leaders	☐	☐	☐	☐	☐
The Holy Spirit	☐	☐	☐	☐	☐
Older established families in the church	☐	☐	☐	☐	☐
You, yourself	☐	☐	☐	☐	☐

5 Where is the focal point of your authority in the church (You may tick as many boxes that you feel apply)

In your position as minister ☐ 1

In your personal 'charisma' ☐ 2

In your expertise ☐ 3

In your calling from God ☐ 4

6 How powerful a person do you perceive yourself to be?

very powerful	☐ 1	not very powerful	☐ 3
moderately powerful	☐ 2	not at all powerful	☐ 4

7 (a) To what extent does your church (as distinct from people) tend to project false expectations on to you?

to a large extent	☐ 1	to some extent	☐ 2	not at all	☐ 3

(b) To what extent does your church attribute to you more authority than is actually yours?

to a large extent	☐ 1	to some extent	☐ 2	not at all	☐ 3

8 How much power do you realistically delegate?

A lot	☐ 1	A moderate amount	☐ 3	Not very much	☐ 4
Quite a lot	☐ 2			None at all	☐ 5

9 How much freedom does your church have to not follow your lead?

A lot	☐ 1	A moderate amount	☐ 3	Not very much	☐ 4
Quite a lot	☐ 2			None at all	☐ 5

10 If you felt very strongly that a course of action was of God, but your church felt otherwise would you:

Accept their decision	☐ 1	Ignore the church's decision	☐ 2

11 How able are you to give way gracefully?

Very able	☐ 1	Able to some extent	☐ 2	Not very able	☐ 3	Not at all able	☐ 4

12 How well are you able to handle anger?

Very able	☐ 1	Able to some extent	☐ 2	Not very able	☐ 3	Not at all able	☐ 4

13 How do you handle disappointment?

Very well	☐ 1	Quite well	☐ 2	Not very well	☐ 3	Not at all well	☐ 4

Relationships Within The Church

1 How well do you relate to:

	Very well	Quite well	Satisfactorily	Not very well	Not at all well
	1	2	3	4	5
your church staff	☐	☐	☐	☐	☐
your assistant minister*	☐	☐	☐	☐	☐
your Lay Leaders/Deacons	☐	☐	☐	☐	☐
your church in general	☐	☐	☐	☐	☐

* your senior minister, if you are the assistant

2 Do you have close friends in your church?

Yes	☐ 1	No	☐ 2

3 If yes, how many close friends do you have in the church?

1-2	☐ 1	3-5	☐ 2	6-8	☐ 3	9+	☐ 4

	Very able	Able to some extent	Not very able	Not at all able
4. How able are you:	1	2	3	4
to speak the truth in love	☐	☐	☐	☐
to receive criticism	☐	☐	☐	☐
to express anger to others	☐	☐	☐	☐
to publicly disagree with others	☐	☐	☐	☐

7

	Yes very much 1	Yes to some extent 2	No - Not really 3	No - Not at all 4
5 Do you think your church is open and honest?	☐	☐	☐	☐
6 Do you enjoy the clash of ideas?	☐	☐	☐	☐
7 Do people find you gentle and compassionate?	☐	☐	☐	☐
8 Are people easily able to disagree with you?	☐	☐	☐	☐
9 Do you tend to sweep issues under the carpet?	☐	☐	☐	☐
10 Do you think people in your church are honest and open with you?	☐	☐	☐	☐
11 Do people tend to find you approachable?	☐	☐	☐	☐
12 Do you tend to confront people with issues?	☐	☐	☐	☐

13 How popular do you think you are in your church?

Very popular	☐ 1	Quite popular	☐ 2	Neither popular nor unpopular	☐ 3	Not very popular	☐ 4	Not at all popular	☐ 5

14 Do you know whether there were any strong objections to your appointment as minister

Yes ☐ 1   No ☐ 2

If yes, what were they?..

Change

Name five key changes which have taken place in your church in the last five years:
PLEASE WRITE IN THE TYPE OF CHANGE UNDER (a), AND THEN FOR EACH CHANGE COMPLETE (b), (c) AND (d).

(a) Change	(b) Who initiated	(c) How decision made	(d) Degree the change has been 'owned' by the church Yes very much 1	Yes to some extent 2	No - Not really 3	No - Not at all 4
1			☐	☐	☐	☐
2			☐	☐	☐	☐
3			☐	☐	☐	☐
4			☐	☐	☐	☐
5			☐	☐	☐	☐

Conflict

1   Is some degree of 'conflict' inevitable in church life?
    Yes   ☐ 1   No   ☐ 2

2   In your experience, can conflict be productive in church life?
    Yes   ☐ 1   No   ☐ 2

3   If yes, in what way(s) can it be productive? ....
    ....

4   Have you in your ministerial career experienced **major** conflict in any church in which you were the minister?
    Yes   ☐ 1   No   ☐ 2

5   We would like you to tell us a bit more about these experiences. (If you have had more than one experience,
    please take the **last two occasions**) - Please describe the incidents, then fill in Q6, 7, 8 and 9 about each one:-

    Occasion 1 ....
    ....
    ....

    Occasion 2 ....
    ....
    ....

		Occasion 1	Occasion 2 (if appropriate)
6	When did the conflict occur:		
	in your present church	☐ 1	☐ 1
	in a past church	☐ 2	☐ 2
7	What did the conflict revolve around (TICK AS MANY AS APPLY):		
	your leadership style	☐ 1	☐ 1
	your values (e.g. mission, worship, theology)	☐ 2	☐ 2
	your competence (e.g. preaching, visiting, counselling)	☐ 3	☐ 3
	your productivity	☐ 4	☐ 4
	some other reason (IF SO STATE)	....	....
		....	....
8	How was the conflict resolved?		
	through compromise	☐ 1	☐ 1
	through acceptance of change	☐ 2	☐ 2
	unresolved	☐ 3	☐ 3
9	Did any members of your church resign as a direct result of the conflict?		
		Yes ☐ 1	Yes ☐ 1
		No ☐ 2	No ☐ 2
	If yes, how many?	....	....

10 Have you ever left a church in unhappy circumstances?
Yes ☐ 1   No ☐ 2

11 If yes,
were you forced to leave? ☐ 1   or   did you leave of your own freewill? ☐ 2

12 As far as you are aware, did your predecessors in your present church ever experience major conflict?
Yes ☐ 1   No ☐ 2   Don't know ☐ 3

13 Have any of your predecessors in your present church left in unhappy circumstances?
Yes ☐ 1   No ☐ 2   Don't know ☐ 3

14 As you think back over the timing of past conflicts, did they erupt:

around Christmas	☐ 1	after the completion of a church building	☐ 6
around Easter	☐ 2	fairly soon after the honeymoon period	☐ 7
around stewardship campaign/budget time	☐ 3	not applicable	☐ 8
after a new member of staff had been appointed	☐ 4	other, WRITE IN......................................	
during a holiday/sabbatical	☐ 5	....	☐ 9

15 Who/what sustains you when you are challenged:

God	☐ 1	friends inside the church	☐ 5
your faith	☐ 2	friends outside the church	☐ 6
your spouse	☐ 3	other, WRITE IN......................................	
your fellow leaders	☐ 4	....	☐ 7

16 Have there been times when you have felt unjustly treated by:
Individuals in the church? ☐ 1   Deacons/Elders ☐ 2   The church itself? ☐ 3

17 If yes, in what areas did you experience this?

overload of expectation	☐ 01	unfair criticism to your face	☐ 07
work overload	☐ 02	unfair criticism behind your back	☐ 08
verbal attacks in a church meeting	☐ 03	sexual manipulation	☐ 09
sidelined, 'ganged up on' by deacons/elders/PCC	☐ 04	threats of dismissal	☐ 10
verbal attacks after a service	☐ 05		
forced into a course of action by influential 'families'/benefactors	☐ 06	others, WRITE IN......................	☐ 11

18 How, and to whom, did you make your anger known? ....
....
....

19 To what extent were you able to let go and forgive?
to a large extent ☐ 1   to some extent ☐ 2   have not been able to forgive ☐ 3

20 As a result of being in the ministry:

	Yes Often 1	Yes Sometimes 2	No 3		Yes often 1	Yes Sometimes 2	No 3
has your health suffered	☐	☐	☐	have you been hurt	☐	☐	☐
have you experienced stress	☐	☐	☐	has your spouse been hurt	☐	☐	☐
have you found sleeping difficult	☐	☐	☐	do you have nightmares	☐	☐	☐
have you had to take anti-depressants	☐	☐	☐	have you ever felt suicidal	☐	☐	☐
does your spouse/family feel you have been abused	☐	☐	☐				

10

21 It has been said *"the church makes a lousy mother"*. Do you agree with this statement?

Yes, very ☐ 1   Yes, to some ☐ 2   No - not ☐ 3   No - Not ☐ 4
much   extent   really   at all

22 Is your preaching aggressive?

often ☐ 1   sometimes ☐ 2   rarely ☐ 3   never ☐ 4

23 Have you lost your temper with the church:

a) in a church service?

often ☐ 1   sometimes ☐ 2   rarely ☐ 3   never ☐ 4

b) in a church meeting?

often ☐ 1   sometimes ☐ 2   rarely ☐ 3   never ☐ 4

24 Have you lost your temper with individuals in the church:

a) in a church service?

often ☐ 1   sometimes ☐ 2   rarely ☐ 3   never ☐ 4

b) in a one-to-one encounter?

often ☐ 1   sometimes ☐ 2   rarely ☐ 3   never ☐ 4

c) in a church meeting?

often ☐ 1   sometimes ☐ 2   rarely ☐ 3   never ☐ 4

25 Have you (& your fellow leaders) been over-zealous in your handling of church discipline?

often ☐ 1   sometimes ☐ 2   rarely ☐ 3   never ☐ 4

Relationships (With The Opposite Sex)

1 Do you have any special guidelines in dealing with members of the opposite sex?

Yes ☐ 1   No ☐ 2

If yes, what are they? ....

....

....

2. Do you counsel members of the opposite sex on your own?

often ☐ 1   sometimes ☐ 2   rarely ☐ 3   never ☐ 4

3 Do you touch or hug members of your church?

often ☐ 1   sometimes ☐ 2   rarely ☐ 3   never ☐ 4

4. Do you believe that ministers are particularly vulnerable to sexual temptation?

Much more than anybody else ☐ 1   About the same as anybody else ☐ 3

A bit more than anybody else ☐ 2   Less vulnerable than most ☐ 4

5. Since you have been in ministry have you found yourself **tempted** to do anything with anyone (not your spouse) that you feel was sexually inappropriate?

often ☐ 1   sometimes ☐ 2   rarely ☐ 3   never ☐ 4

6. Since you have been in ministry, have you ever **done** anything with someone (not your spouse) that you feel was sexually inappropriate?

often ☐ 1   sometimes ☐ 2   rarely ☐ 3   never ☐ 4

11

Thank you for taking time and helping out with this valuable survey. When this survey has been completed we may want to contact some ministers again, for a more in-depth, face to face interview on this subject. Would you be willing to be considered for further research?

Yes ☐ 1   No ☐ 2

If you have any further comments on the subject, or the questionnaire, please write them below or on a separate sheet and return them with your questionnaire in the stamped addressed envelope provided.

Thank you again for your time and trouble.

Linda

LINDA JONES

Appendix Two
(*Church Officers*)

Leadership Styles - Church Officers Questionnaire
PLEASE TICK BOX OR WRITE IN ANSWER - WHICHEVER IS APPLICABLE

1 Position Held:
   Church Warden ☐ 1   Secretary ☐ 2   Treasurer ☐ 3

Classification Data

2 Name ....

3 Sex:
   Male ☐ 1   Female ☐ 2

4 Age:
    < 30 ☐ 1   45-54 ☐ 3   65+ ☐ 5
   31-44 ☐ 2   55-64 ☐ 4

5 Occupation ....

6 Number of years you have belonged to your present church:
   10 or under ☐ 1   21-30 ☐ 3   41 + ☐ 5
   11-20   ☐ 2   31-40 ☐ 4

7 Number of years you have held present office .... _____ years

8 Have you held other offices in this church?
   Yes ☐ 1   No ☐ 2
   If yes, please specify below, and write in number of years you held the office for. (The office(s) held need not necessarily be restricted to those mentioned in question 1.)

Office Held	Number of Years
1.	
2.	
3.	

9 Have you ever belonged to another church?
   Yes ☐ 1   No ☐ 2

   If yes, did you ever hold office in that church(es)?
   Yes ☐ 1   No ☐ 2

   If yes, please specify below and write in number of years you held office for.

Office Held	Number of Years
1.	
2.	
3.	

10 a. What is the theological position of your church (you may tick more than one box)?

Fundamentalist ☐ 1   Middle of the road ☐ 3   Charismatic ☐ 5
Evangelical ☐ 2   Liberal ☐ 4   Catholic ☐ 6

10 b. What is your own theological position?

Fundamentalist ☐ 1   Middle of the road ☐ 3   Charismatic ☐ 5
Evangelical ☐ 2   Liberal ☐ 4   Catholic ☐ 6

11 How ambitious are you?

very ambitious ☐ 1   fairly ambitious ☐ 2   not very ambitious ☐ 3   not at all ambitious ☐ 4

12 How competitive are you?

very ☐ 1   quite ☐ 2   not very ☐ 3   not at all ☐ 4

Involvement In Church Work

13 (a) In an average week, what is the **total** number of hours you work for the church _____ hours

(b) How **many hours** in an average week do you give to each of the following activities (WRITE IN BELOW)

(c) What do you **enjoy** most in your church work? Please give each item listed an enjoyment rating out of 10.
(i.e. 10 = Maximum enjoyment, 0 = minimum enjoyment)

	Q 13(b) Number of Hours	Q 13(c) Rating out of 10
administration		
committees		
community involvement/social action		
counselling		
discipling/nurturing		
enabling/involving the laity in ministry		
evangelism		
prayer and meditation		
lay preaching		
study		
visiting - building & maintaining meaningful relationships		
worship preparation/leading worship		

14a) Has your church developed a 'mission statement'?

Yes ☐ 1   No ☐ 2

14b) If yes, please state it ....
....

15 To what extent do you see your church actively fulfilling that mission statement?

totally ☐ 1   for the most part ☐ 2   not at all ☐ 3

16 In Church meetings to what extent does the "agenda" revolve around issues of mission rather than issues of maintenance (finance, fabric, etc.)?

Totally mission ☐ 1   ¼ mission, ¾ maintenance ☐ 4
¾ mission, ¼ maintenance ☐ 2   Totally maintenance ☐ 5
½ mission, ½ maintenance ☐ 3

Leadership Style Of Your Minister

1 Which of the following personality types do you consider your minister (senior if more than one) to be?

High-key, aggressive ☐ 1   Middle of the road, neither high or low-key ☐ 2   Low-key, laid-back ☐ 3

2 Which of the following best describes his/her leadership style?

autocratic ☐ 1   persuasive ☐ 2   consultative ☐ 3   participative ☐ 4

3　(a)　Does he/she more often try to:
　　　help people say what they think　☐ 1　**or**　says what he/she thinks right away?　☐ 2

　　(b)　Does he/she have a clear sense of vision for the life of your church?
　　　Yes　☐ 1　　　　No　☐ 2

　　If so, please sum up his/her sense of vision in one sentence (if you can!):..
　　...

4　To whom in **theory** is your minister accountable?...

5　To whom in **practise** is your minister accountable? ....

6　Does he/she have a formal job description?
　　Yes　☐ 1　　　　No　☐ 2　　　　Don't Know　☐ 3

The Structure of Power In The Church

1a) Please tick the box which most reflects your agreement/disagreement with these statements.

	Agree Strongly	Agree slightly	Neither Agree nor Disagree	Disagree slightly	Disagree Strongly
	1	2	3	4	5
"God wants us to be powerful because there is a lot God wants us to do"	☐	☐	☐	☐	☐
"Power is not a dirty word. It is the ability to mobilise resources"	☐	☐	☐	☐	☐
"The exercise of power can only be justified in the interests of empowering others"	☐	☐	☐	☐	☐
"Power is like saltwater: the more you drink the thirstier you become"	☐	☐	☐	☐	☐
"Power tends to corrupt, and absolute power corrupts absolutely, and this is especially true of religion"	☐	☐	☐	☐	☐
"Resorting to piety is a power play peculiar to Christians"	☐	☐	☐	☐	☐
"The exercise of power always implies coercion and violence"	☐	☐	☐	☐	☐
"Power is a serious problem in the church today"	☐	☐	☐	☐	☐

1b) Please tick the box which most reflects your agreement/disagreement with these statements.

	Agree Strongly	Agree slightly	Neither Agree nor Disagree	Disagree slightly	Disagree Strongly
	1	2	3	4	5
"Ministers exercise too much power"	☐	☐	☐	☐	☐
"Ministers need to delegate more"	☐	☐	☐	☐	☐
"Ministers need to be people-orientated, not goal-orientated"	☐	☐	☐	☐	☐
"Pastoral leadership is non-coercive"	☐	☐	☐	☐	☐
"Personal growth is more important than church growth"	☐	☐	☐	☐	☐
"Ministers have a God-given authority to lead"	☐	☐	☐	☐	☐
"Churches benefit from strong leadership"	☐	☐	☐	☐	☐
"The key to church growth is leadership"	☐	☐	☐	☐	☐
"Ministers should not be afraid to use their power"	☐	☐	☐	☐	☐
"Good pastoral leadership is directive"	☐	☐	☐	☐	☐

3

2 How does your minister tend to exercise power? Is it:
   'over' people as he/she gives a strong lead ☐ 1
   'within' the church by inspiration of his/her personality ☐ 2
   'with' people as he/she in turn empowers them ☐ 3

3. To what extent do you feel that your minister has been involved in doing any of the following?

	Very often 1	Fairly often 2	Rarely 3	Never 4
imposing his/her own style of worship	☐	☐	☐	☐
using his/her sexuality to help him/her get his/her own way	☐	☐	☐	☐
being manipulative in church meetings in order to get his/her own way	☐	☐	☐	☐
not providing a lead when it is needed	☐	☐	☐	☐
pushing through a course of action that was unpopular	☐	☐	☐	☐
playing on the guilt of members of the congregation	☐	☐	☐	☐
'hiding behind God' in order to get his/her own way	☐	☐	☐	☐
intimidating weaker people into a course of action	☐	☐	☐	☐

4 Please tick the box which in your view best describes the strength of power exerted by each of the following groups of people in your church:

	Very strong 1	Strong 2	Neither Strong nor Weak 3	Weak 4	Very Weak 5
Congregation/Church meeting	☐	☐	☐	☐	☐
Elders/Deacons/PCC	☐	☐	☐	☐	☐
Former leaders	☐	☐	☐	☐	☐
The Holy Spirit	☐	☐	☐	☐	☐
Older established families in the church	☐	☐	☐	☐	☐
The Minister	☐	☐	☐	☐	☐

5 Where is the focal point of ministerial authority in your church (You may tick as many boxes that you feel apply)
   In his/her position as minister ☐ 1   In his/her expertise ☐ 3
   In his/her personal 'charisma' ☐ 2   In his/her calling from God ☐ 4

6 How powerful a person do you perceive your minister to be?
   very powerful ☐ 1   not very powerful ☐ 3
   moderately powerful ☐ 2   not at all powerful ☐ 4

7 (a) To what extent does your church (as distinct from people) tend to project false expectations on to your minister?
   to a large extent ☐ 1   to some extent ☐ 2   not at all ☐ 3

   (b) To what extent does your church attribute to him/her more authority than he/she actually has?
   to a large extent ☐ 1   to some extent ☐ 2   not at all ☐ 3

8 How much power does he/she realistically delegate?
   A lot ☐ 1   A moderate amount ☐ 3   Not very much ☐ 4
   Quite a lot ☐ 2   None at all ☐ 5

9 How much freedom does your church have to not follow his/her lead?
   A lot ☐ 1   A moderate amount ☐ 3   Not very much ☐ 4
   Quite a lot ☐ 2   None at all ☐ 5

4

10 If he/she felt very strongly that a course of action was of God, but your church felt otherwise, do you think he/she would:

Accept their decision   ❏ 1   Ignore the church's decision   ❏ 2

11 How able is he/she to give way gracefully?

Very able   ❏ 1   Able to some extent   ❏ 2   Not very able   ❏ 3   Not at all able   ❏ 4

12 How well is he/she able to handle anger?

Very able   ❏ 1   Able to some extent   ❏ 2   Not very able   ❏ 3   Not at all able   ❏ 4

13 How does he/she handle disappointment?

Very well   ❏ 1   Quite well   ❏ 2   Not very well   ❏ 3   Not at all well   ❏ 4

Your Minister And Relationships Within The Church

1 How well does your minister relate to:

	Very well 1	Quite well 2	Satisfactorily 3	Not very well 4	Not at all well 5
the church staff	❏	❏	❏	❏	❏
the assistant minister	❏	❏	❏	❏	❏
the Lay Leaders/Deacons	❏	❏	❏	❏	❏
the church in general	❏	❏	❏	❏	❏

2. How able is he/she:

	Very able 1	Able to some extent 2	Not very able 3	Not at all able 4
to speak the truth in love	❏	❏	❏	❏
to receive criticism	❏	❏	❏	❏
to express anger to others	❏	❏	❏	❏
to publicly disagree with others	❏	❏	❏	❏

	Yes very much 1	Yes to some extent 2	No - Not really 3	No - Not at all 4
3 Do you think your church is open and honest with your minister?	❏	❏	❏	❏
4 Does he/she enjoy the clash of ideas?	❏	❏	❏	❏
5 Do people find him/her gentle and compassionate?	❏	❏	❏	❏
6 Are people easily able to disagree with him/her?	❏	❏	❏	❏
7 Does he/she tend to sweep issues under the carpet?	❏	❏	❏	❏
8 Do people tend to find him/her approachable?	❏	❏	❏	❏
9 Does he/she tend to confront people with issues?	❏	❏	❏	❏

10 How popular do you think your minister is with members of your church?

Very popular   ❏ 1   Quite popular   ❏ 2   Neither popular nor unpopular   ❏ 3   Not very popular   ❏ 4   Not at all popular   ❏ 5

11 Do you know whether there were any strong objections to his/her appointment as minister

Yes   ❏ 1   No   ❏ 2

If yes, what were they?..

5

Change

Name five **key** changes which have taken place in your church in the last five years:
PLEASE WRITE IN THE TYPE OF CHANGE UNDER (a), AND THEN FOR EACH CHANGE COMPLETE (b), (c) AND (d).

	(a) Change	(b) Who initiated	(c) How decision made	(d) Degree the change has been 'owned' by the church			
				Yes very much 1	Yes to some extent 2	No - Not really 3	No - Not at all 4
1				❏	❏	❏	❏
2				❏	❏	❏	❏
3				❏	❏	❏	❏
4				❏	❏	❏	❏
5				❏	❏	❏	❏

Conflict

1 Is some degree of 'conflict' inevitable in church life?
   Yes ❏ 1   No ❏ 2

2 In your experience, can conflict be productive in church life?
   Yes ❏ 1   No ❏ 2

3 If yes, in what way(s) can it be productive? ....
....

4 Has **any** minister experienced **major** conflict in **any** church to which you have belonged?
   Yes ❏ 1   No ❏ 2   Don't Know ❏ 3

5 We would like you to tell us a bit more about these experiences. (If you have had more than one experience, please take the **last two occasions**) - Please describe the incidents, then fill in Q6, 7, 8 and 9 about each one:-

   Occasion 1 ....
   ....

   Occasion 2 ....
   ....

6

		Occasion 1	Occasion 2 (if appropriate)

6 When did the conflict occur:
  in your present church — ❏ 1 — ❏ 1
  in a past church — ❏ 2 — ❏ 2

7 What did the conflict revolve around (TICK AS MANY AS APPLY):
  leadership style of the minister — ❏ 1 — ❏ 1
  the minister's values (e.g. in terms mission, worship, theology) — ❏ 2 — ❏ 2
  his/her competence (e.g. preaching, visiting, counselling) — ❏ 3 — ❏ 3
  his/her productivity — ❏ 4 — ❏ 4
  some other reason (IF SO STATE) ....

  ....

8 How was the conflict resolved?
  through compromise — ❏ 1 — ❏ 1
  through acceptance of change — ❏ 2 — ❏ 2
  unresolved — ❏ 3 — ❏ 3

9 Did any members of the church resign as a direct result of the conflict?
  Yes ❏ 1 — Yes ❏ 1
  No ❏ 2 — No ❏ 2

  If yes, how many? ....

10 Has **any** minister ever left a church, to which you belonged, in unhappy circumstances?
  Yes ❏ 1   No ❏ 2

11 If yes,
  was he/she forced to leave? ❏ 1   **or**   did he/she leave of his/her own freewill? ❏ 2

12 As far as you are aware, did any previous ministers in your present church ever experience major conflict?
  Yes ❏ 1   No ❏ 2   Don't know ❏ 3

13 Have any of the ministers in your present church left in unhappy circumstances?
  Yes ❏ 1   No ❏ 2   Don't know ❏ 3

14 As you think back over the timing of past conflicts, did they erupt:
  around Christmas ❏ 1 — after the completion of a church building ❏ 6
  around Easter ❏ 2 — fairly soon after the honeymoon period ❏ 7
  around stewardship campaign/budget time ❏ 3 — not applicable ❏ 8
  after a new member of staff had been appointed ❏ 4 — other, WRITE IN.....................................
  during a holiday/sabbatical ❏ 5 — .... ❏ 9

15 Have there been times when you have felt that **any** minister has been unjustly treated by:
  Individuals in the church? ❏ 1   Deacons/Elders ❏ 2   The church itself? ❏ 3

16 If yes, in what areas did the minister experience this?
  overload of expectation ❏ 01 — unfair criticism to his/her face ❏ 07
  work overload ❏ 02 — unfair criticism behind his/her back ❏ 08
  verbal attacks in a church meeting ❏ 03 — sexual manipulation ❏ 09
  sidelined, 'ganged up on' by deacons/elders/PCC ❏ 04 — threats of dismissal ❏ 10
  verbal attacks after a service ❏ 05
  forced into a course of action by influential 'families'/benefactors ❏ 06 — others, WRITE IN...
  .... ❏ 11

7

17 How, and to whom, did he/she make his/her anger known? ....

....

....

18 To what extent was he/she able to let go and forgive?

to a large extent ☐ 1   to some extent   ☐ 2   has not been able to forgive   ☐ 3

19 Are you aware of **any** minister experiencing any of the following, as a result of being in ministry?

	Yes Often 1	Yes Sometimes 2	No 3		Yes often 1	Yes Sometimes 2	No 3
suffered ill health	☐	☐	☐	been hurt	☐	☐	☐
experienced stress	☐	☐	☐	had nightmares	☐	☐	☐
found sleeping difficult	☐	☐	☐	ever felt suicidal	☐	☐	☐
had to take anti-depressants	☐	☐	☐	felt his/her spouse has been hurt	☐	☐	☐
felt that his/her spouse/family have been abused	☐	☐	☐				

20 It has been said *"the church makes a lousy mother"*. Do you agree with this statement?

Yes, very ☐ 1   Yes, to some ☐ 2   No - not   ☐ 3   No - Not ☐ 4
much   extent   really   at all

21 Is your minister's preaching aggressive?

often   ☐ 1   sometimes ☐ 2   rarely ☐ 3   never   ☐ 4

22 Has he/she lost his/her temper with the church:

a) in a church service?

often   ☐ 1   sometimes ☐ 2   rarely ☐ 3   never   ☐ 4

b) in a church meeting?

often   ☐ 1   sometimes ☐ 2   rarely ☐ 3   never   ☐ 4

23 Has he/she lost his/her temper with individuals in the church:

a) in a church service?

often   ☐ 1   sometimes ☐ 2   rarely ☐ 3   never   ☐ 4

b) in a one-to-one encounter?

often   ☐ 1   sometimes ☐ 2   rarely ☐ 3   never   ☐ 4

c) in a church meeting?

often   ☐ 1   sometimes ☐ 2   rarely ☐ 3   never   ☐ 4

24 Has he/she (& your fellow leaders) been over-zealous in their handling of church discipline?

often   ☐ 1   sometimes ☐ 2   rarely ☐ 3   never   ☐ 4

Thank you for taking time and helping out with this valuable survey.

If you have any further comments on the subject, or the questionnaire, please write them on a separate sheet and return them with your questionnaire in the stamped addressed envelope provided.

Thank you again for your time and trouble.

Linda

LINDA JONES

8

Bibliography

Avis, Paul, *Authority, Leadership and Conflict in the Church*, (London: Mowbray, 1992)

Barna, George, *Today's Pastors*, (Ventura California: Regal, 1993)

Bash, Anthony, *Ambassadors for Christ: An Exploration of Ambassadorial Language in the New Testament*, (Tübingen: JCB Mohr, 1997)

Beasley-Murray, Paul, *A Call to Excellence*, (London: Hodder & Stoughton, 1995)

Beasley-Murray, Paul, *Dynamic Leadership*, (Eastbourne: Monarch, 1990)

Biggar, Nigel, 'Power And Powerlessness' 141–152 in *Pastoral Ethics*, ed. D. Atkinson, (Oxford: Lynx, 1994)

Buchanan, Deans, 'Ministry and Suffering in the Life of Paul', *Ministry Today* 8 (October 1996) 6–26

Buzzard, Lynn, 'War and Peace in the Local Church', *Leadership* IV.3 (Summer 1983) 20–30

Jackson, W. Caroll, *As One With Authority: Reflective Leadership in Ministry*, (Louisville, Kentucky: Westminster/John Knox Press, 1991)

Center For Leadership Studies, *Power Perception Profile*, distributed in Europe by Management Learning Resources Ltd, PO Box 28, Carmarthen, Dyfed SA31 1DT

Dobson, Edward G., Speed, B. Leas & Marshall, Shelley, *Mastering Conflict and Controversy*, (Portland, Oregon: Multnomah Press, 1992)

Enroth, Ronald M., *Churches That Abuse*, (Grand Rapids, Michigan: Zondervan, 1992)

Falbo, Toni, New, B. Lynn & Gaines,Margie, 'Perceptions of Authority and the Power Strategies used by Clergymen', *Journal for the Scientific Study of Religion* 26.4 (December 1987) 499–507

Forbes, Cheryl, *The Religion of Power*, (Bromley: English edition Marc Europe, 1986)

Foster, Richard, *Money, Sex and Power*, (London: English edition Hodder & Stoughton, 1985)

Fouque, Patricia, 'Abuse in Ministry', *Ministry Today* 10 (June 1997) 7–13

Gafke Art & McSpadden Bruce with Laird, Rebecca 'Power Principles for Pastors', *Congregations* (July–August 1994) 10–13

Gregory, Joel, *Too Great a Temptation: the Seductive Power of America's Super Church*, (Fort Worth, Texas: The Summit Group, 1994)

Guggenbuhl-Craig, Adolf, *Power in the Helping Professions*, (Dallas, Texas: Spring Publications, 1971)

Hahn, Celia Allison, *Growing in Authority, Relinquishing Control: A New Approach to Faithful Leadership*, (Bethesda, Maryland: Alban, 1994)

Hahn, Celia Allison, 'The Paradoxical Authority of Clergy: Four Stories', *Congregations* (July–August 1994) 14–18

Hammond, Phillip E., Salinas, Luis, & Sloane, Douglas, 'Types of Clergy Authority: Their Measurement, Location and Effects', *Journal for the Scientific Study of Religion* 17.3 (Sept 1978) 241–253

Harris, John C., *Stress, Power and Ministry*, (Bethesda, Maryland: Alban, 1977)

Hengel, Martin, *Christ and Power*, (Belfast & Dublin: E.T. Christian Journals, 1977)

Holloway, Richard & Avery Brice, *Churches and How to Survive Them*, (London: HarperCollins, 1994)

Horton, Michael Scott (ed.), *Power Religion: The Selling Out of the Evangelical Church?* (Chicago: Moody Press, 1992)

Howard, Roland, *The Rise and Fall of the Nine O'Clock Service*, (London: Cassell, 1996)

Hybels, Bill, 'Standing in the Crossfire' *Leadership* XIV.1 (Winter 1993) 14–22

Ingram Larry C., 'Notes On Pastoral Power In The Congregational Tradition', *Journal for the Scientific Study of Religion* 19.1 (March 1980) 40–48

Ingram Larry C., 'Leadership, Democracy And Religion: Role Ambiguity Among Pastors in Southern Baptist Churches', *Journal for the Scientific Study of Religion* 20.2 (June 1981) 119–129

Jinks, Michael & Deborah B., *Power and Change in Parish Ministry*, (Washington DC: Alban Institute, 1991)

Leas, Speed B., *Leadership and Conflict*, (Nashville: Abingdon Press, 1982)

Leas, Speed B., 'Inside Church Fights', *Leadership* X.1 (Winter 1989) 12–20

Mackey, James, *Power and Christian Ethics*, (Cambridge: Cambridge University Press, 1994)

Malony, H. Newton & Hunt, Richard A., *The Psychology of Clergy*, (Harrisburg PA: Morehouse Publishing, 1991)

May, Rollo, *Power and Innocence: A Search for the Sources of Violence*, (Glasgow: British edition Fontana/Collins, 1976)

Nouwen, Henri J.M., *The Path of Power* (London: E.T. British edition DLT, 1995)

Oswald, Roy M., *Power Analysis of A Congregation*, (Bethesda, Maryland: Alban Paper, 1981)

Patterson, Ben, 'A Small Pump at the Edge of the Swamp: When the alligators are snapping, how do you operate?', *Leadership* I.2 (Spring 1980) 29–34

Percy, Martyn, *Words, Wonders and Power: Understanding Contemporary Christian Fundamentalism and Revivalism*, (London: SPCK 1996)

Percy, Martyn, *Power and the Church: Ecclesiology in an Age of Transition*, (London: Cassell, 1997)

Poling, James Newton, *The Abuse of Power: A Theological Problem*, (Nashville: Abingdon Press, 1991)

Price, Roy, 'Building Trust Between a Pastor and Congregation', *Leadership* I.2 (Spring 1980) 35–41

Purvis, Sally B., *The Power of the Cross: Foundations for a Christian Feminist Ethic of Community*, (Nashville: Abingdon Press, 1993)

Reed, Bruce, *The Dynamics of Religion: Process and Movement in Christian Churches*, (London: Darton, Longman & Todd, 1978)

Roberts, Richard H., 'Lord, Bondsman and Churchman: Identity, Integrity and Power in Anglicanism' 156–224 in *On Being the Church: Essays On the Christian Community* (Edinburgh: T & T Clark, 1989) edited by C.E. Gunton & D.W. Hardy

Rogers, Carl, *On Personal Power*, (London: British edition Constable, 1978)

Ross, Alistair, *Evangelicals in Exile*, (London: Darton, Longman & Todd, 1997)

Runcie, Robert, *Authority in Crisis? An Anglican Response*, SCM, London 1988

Salter, Darius, *What Really Happens in Ministry: Profiling Pastoral Success in Flourishing Churches*, (Grand Rapids, Michigan: Baker Book House, 1990)

Schnase, Robert, *Ambition in Ministry: Our Spiritual Struggle with Success, Achievement and Competition*, (Nashville: Abingdon Press, 1993)

Sipe, A.W. Richard, *Sex, Priests and Power: Anatomy of a Crisis*, (London: Cassell, 1995)

Skinner, John E., 'Ideology, Authority and Faith' 27–46 in *Authority in the Anglican Communion* ed. Sykes, Stephen W., (Toronto: Anglican Book Centre, 1987)

Stevens, R. Paul & Collins, Phil, *The Equipping Pastor: A Systems Approach to Congregational Leadership*, (Bethesda, Maryland: Alban Institute, 1993)

Stortz, Martha Ellen, *PastorPower*, (Nashville: Abingdon Press, 1993)

Taylor, James, 'The Spirituality of Weakness', *Baptist Ministers Journal* 258 (April 1997) 3–7

Tournier, Paul, *The Violence Inside*, (London: E.T. SCM, 1978)

Walker, Arlo (pseudonym), 'Are Pastors Abused?' *Leadership* XIV.1 (Winter 1993) 80–84

Watts, Fraser, 'Enabling Authority: A Psychological Approach', *Modern Churchman* (NS) 33.2 (1991)11–19

Wink, Walter, *Engaging the Powers: Discernment and Resistance in a World of Domination*, (Minneapolis: Fortress Press, 1992)